# FORD
# MUSTANG
## The First Generation

# CLIVE BRANSON

AMBERLEY

*This book is dedicated to all those with a rumble in their souls
and oil in their veins.*

Clive Branson

*Title page*: 1968 Mustang Fastback. (Clive Branson)

First published 2019

Amberley Publishing
The Hill, Stroud
Gloucestershire, GL5 4EP

www.amberley-books.com

Copyright © Clive Branson, 2019

The right of Clive Branson to be identified as the Author
of this work has been asserted in accordance with the
Copyrights, Designs and Patents Act 1988.

British Library Cataloguing in Publication Data.
A catalogue record for this book is available from the British Library.

ISBN: 978 1 4456 8788 9 (print)
ISBN: 978 1 4456 8789 6 (ebook)

Typeset in 11pt on 13pt Sabon.
Typesetting by Aura Technology and Software Services, India.
Printed in the UK.

# CONTENTS

# INTRODUCTION

Although independent car manufacturers, such as Kaiser, Kurtis, Packard, Crosley and Cunningham, had American sports cars on the roads prior to the mid-1950s, they received a guarded reception from the public. It was the GI returning from the Second World War in Europe who actually introduced (or perhaps forced) the sports car craze into America's mainstream consciousness, but reputation takes a while to establish and manufacturers, like the conservative Big Three in Detroit, wouldn't change tactics unless there was overwhelming consensus from the general public. The impression that sports cars gave was one of fun but frivolity. A car measured a man's status. To be taken seriously, building anything smaller than a PT boat was simply un-American and changing tactics was unthinkable.

A car's shape can make it an object of desire, even a temple of worship. Whether hotly contested or not, everyone has an opinion about cars, even those who say they pay little regard to them. The Mustang changed all that. Ford introduced a car that was made for the track circuit and for the city tarmac. It was affordable, sexy, streamlined and everyone, from the CEO to the hairdresser, looked good in it. Suddenly, driving wasn't so much about getting to the destination but about the journey itself. When Ford introduced the Mustang in 1964 at the New York World's Fair, it unshackled all preconceived restraints as to how an American car should look. The Mustang, though limited by budget restraints, was a car built by a group of guys in white shirts and thin ties using slide rules, who built a car based on passion. Not only was it the financial life raft for the Ford Motor Company, it became its flagship. It was conceived, built and packaged by the right people, at the right time, doing the right thing.

Between 1979 and 2004 (the Mustang's third and fourth generations), Ford became complacent with its Mustang designs, adopting caution, competing against the ubiquitous smaller Asian cars, and departing from what gave the Mustang such presence. Though these models performed well, and were unquestionably powerful and economical, aesthetically they were rather listless. Ford designers had to acquiesce to restrictions concerning safety, emission control and fuel consumption, forcing limitations on the unique styling. Ironically, today's car designs have done a complete circle, the car becoming more of a utilitarian vehicle designed by computer analysis, committee decisions, financial restrictions and environmental regulations, pushing all thoughts about their character to the background as form follows function. As a result, cars are almost indistinguishable and this drought has led to a visceral feeling, especially from car enthusiasts, expressing a hankering for those halcyon days when cars exuded a sense of soul, character and individuality. Fortunately, the Ford Mustang has returned to the retro look of what made the brand so appealing – compact power and styling.

For the most part, cars are designed as an identity, a resonant facsimile of the era, on par with music and fashion. They reflect the tone of social values, desires and vision. In very rare cases, certain car brands are more than mere steel, plastic and glass, but a metaphor that breaks all conventionality. It surpasses the rudimentary role of transportation and embraces an opiate love affair with the people. These cars force the world to take notice. One such revelation was a watershed moment for Ford and the automotive world called the Ford Mustang.

This book is about such a car and, in particular, the first generation of Mustangs (1964–73), which is the most influential Mustang generation in terms of styling, innovation, and variety, as well as the most sought after models for collectors and enthusiasts. Time is impervious on a classic. Hope you enjoy the ride.

# 1

# PERFECT TIMING

The aftermath of the Second World War saw America, the new capitalist frontier, bloom with a feeling of invincibility, affluence and optimism about the future, and this confidence was reflected in an attitude that bigger was better, including the size and design of American cars. The dawning of the Space Age and the Space Race had a huge impact on contemporary American automotive styling and lifestyle, expanding suburbanisation, the mall and the decline of the inner city. Their cars were big, garish and vulgar, oozing with glittering chrome.

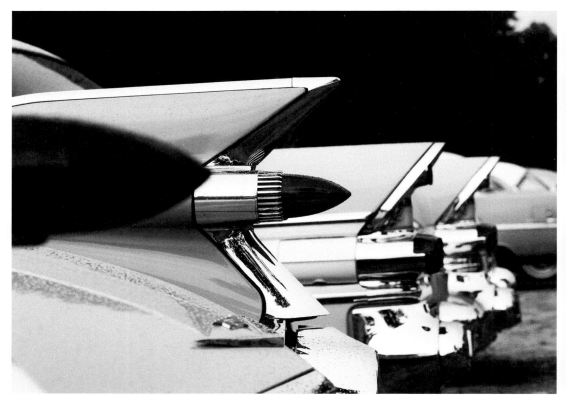

Cadillacs. (Clive Branson)

There were cavernous, wide, snarling, open-mouthed grills, aeronautic shaped wings and hoods the length of an RV. Underneath lay a gargantuan V8 motor housed in a bungalow-sized torso of a car.

In 1950 there were 40 million cars on American roads. By the end of the decade that number would almost double. The car became the nucleus of America's psyche and by the end of the 1950s auto industries employed, either directly or indirectly, one in six working Americans.[1] The United States became the industrial leader – the car was king, catapulting the country into position as the world's largest manufacturer of automobiles. It was a euphoric time when profitability and jobs paved the future and the euphemism for cheapness was 'Made in Japan'. By the early 1960s, car designs had changed from ostentatious and bulbous to stretched and angular. Needless to say, imports had their revenge and models from the likes of MG, Triumph, Austin-Healey, Jaguar, Fiat, Volvo and VW cut into domestic profits. These cars were small, nimble, fun and full of character. To thwart such competition, Detroit's Big Three manufacturers spat out a rash of square-shaped versions of compacts such as Ford's Falcon, Chevrolet's Corvair (the first rear-engine American-made car), Plymouth's Valiant, Dodge's Dart, Lincoln-Mercury's Comet, Oldsmobile's F-85, Pontiac's Tempest and Buick's Special. Though these cars could be described as about as memorable as the morning cereal, this emphasis on smaller American cars achieved the desired sharp drop in domestic import sales. At the time, US buyers had 266 different models to choose from, ranging from the standard priced Rambler American sedan at just under $2,000 to the exclusive Cadillac Eldorado Brougham at the exorbitant price of $13,000 (the price of a middle-class house). By comparison, the median family income in 1960 was $5,620. Furthermore, the tax levied on a vehicle was about one-third of a car's price.

The early 1960s were a hedonistic time, when most Americans were still revelling in the surfeit of 1950s prosperity, privilege, innocence and optimism reflected in superhighways, cheap oil, the inspiration of John F. Kennedy, the Beatles and space exploration. Yet underneath the tranquillity and reserved placidity there was an iconoclastic rumbling of discontent. When it surfaced in the mid-1960s, this discontent exploded into a period of tumultuous conflict and rebellion: politically, socially and culturally. Sexual liberation, experimentation in fashion, music, literature and education, artistic expression and the emergence of flower power: all met with equally virulent opposition. In just four years, America was embroiled in a Cold War, potential nuclear annihilation with the Soviet Union, the Vietnam War, a threatening oil crisis, the deaths of icons John F. Kennedy and Marilyn Monroe, the emergence of the Black Panthers and racial and sexual confrontation.

# 2

# Trouble in Paradise

The 1950s is arguably the decade in which American auto manufacturers regurgitated some of the most exaggerated and garish cars in history. At least the bland 1940s had an excuse – restraint due to the war – but there was no excuse in the 1950s except for the propensity to self-indulgence. Vying against each other in frenzied envy, designers applied as many wings, fins, barnacles, panelling, excess and excuses, and as much chrome, as they could to a vehicle. Automobiles dripped in ornaments rather than practical design. Such ostentation eventually became a manufacturer's Achilles heel as the public

1958 Ford Edsel Ranger two-door. (Clive Branson)

grew weary of these pretentious gas-guzzlers and Ford's newly released Edsel, named after Henry Ford's son and introduced in the summer of 1957, merely confirmed the backlash.

It certainly wasn't because of a lack of innovation. Hyped as 'the car with a difference', the Edsel indisputably was that. It was stuffed with gadgets from self-adjusting brakes and automatic lubrication to push-button, automatic transmission controls that were housed in the hub of the steering column, only for drivers to be confused, assuming it was part of the horn. Ford estimated that it would need to sell 200,000 Edsels just to break even; alas, the only thing it achieved was public derision, ridicule and scorn while press reviews were hostile. Within weeks of the Edsel's release, the media discovered that the car was as riddled with problems as Bonnie and Clyde's car was with bullet holes. The obvious flaws were inferior paint jobs, low-grade sheet metal and non-functioning accessories. The more it was criticized, the more controversial it became.

Critics referred to its grille as a 'horsecollar' or lampooned it for resembling a toilet seat or, more crudely, the female genitalia.[2] It was a catastrophe and during its tenure generated losses estimated to reach between $250 million to $400 million (in production and in marketing attempts to revive a dead horse), bankrupting many Ford dealerships.[3] Needless to say, it didn't help matters when you had quotes from the likes of John Brooks in *Business Adventures*: 'It did not help that they were delivered with oil leaks, sticking hoods, trunks that wouldn't open, and push buttons that couldn't be budged with a hammer.'[4]

The Age of Excessiveness, economically and aesthetically, was over. Americans were facing the Eisenhower recession, forcing consumers to seek smaller, economic cars, such as the Volkswagen Beetle. The Edsel, in response, was simply the wrong product, at the wrong time, for all the wrong reasons, and aimed at the wrong audience. In hindsight, the decline was more than bad taste: it was a combination of bad marketing, bad quality and bad timing. The Big Three US automakers had become complacent and smug in building second-rate leviathans while losing touch with the current trend. A car like the Edsel might have done better had it been sold to Eastern Europe or Cuba. Only 109,000 Edsels were sold in less than three years of production. Their crippling results became known as one of the biggest flops in automotive history. It was the very nadir of Ford's history and the company was floundering from a Titanic-sized disaster.

The present is always moulded by the past, so let's step back to how all of this came about. In 1945, Henry Ford II inherited the Ford Motor Company; Henry Ford's son, Edsel, had died in 1943 from stomach cancer. Thanks to his grandfather's autocratic obstinacy in making poor decisions and a penchant for hiring sycophants, Henry Ford II was left with a diseased and almost insolvent company. No one even knew how the bookkeeping was done. Henry Ford was seventy-eight years old and suffering from heart problems and atherosclerosis, not to mention deteriorating mental health, contributing to numerous erratic decisions.[5] Though Henry Ford was forced to relinquish the reins, the damage was already done, leaving Henry Ford II in desperate need of help. Fortuitously, he received a telegram from Robert McNamara and eight of his economist colleagues from Harvard, claiming they could save his company. Henry Ford II had no alternative but to hire this group, known by their university fraternity as the 'Whiz Kids'.[6] Over the next decade, the Whiz Kids put themselves on a diverging course from the hierarchy of the company. For one thing, they had no interest in cars per se. The Whiz Kids were the vanguard of an emerging philosophical movement in business, expressing a style that emphasized bottom-line productivity rather than an emphasis on style itself. It was a dramatic shift for the Ford Motor Company and often difficult since the company had been dominated throughout most of its history by its founder's deeply held (and arbitrary) convictions about how cars should be designed and built, even when that approach was not the cheapest or easiest route.[7] The Whiz Kids transformed Ford's inner workings, instituting modern financial controls, developing the company's first real system of internal audits and bringing order to production planning and cash-flow management.[8]

Henry Ford II. (National Automotive History Collection, Detroit Public Library)

Among the Whiz Kids, none ascended faster in the company than Robert McNamara. McNamara became Ford's controller in mid-1948 and by January 1955 he was vice president and general manager of Ford Division. In May 1957, he became group vice president, responsible for all of the company's car and truck divisions. As bright as McNamara was, he wasn't a 'people person'. His zeal focused on the coldness of mathematics, systems and attention to detail, often sacrificing aesthetics to parsimoniousness. And though he was viewed internally as a technocrat, his methods proved profitable when it came to the production of the Ford Skyliner and the Lincoln Continental, even the unimaginable enlarging of the cherished two-seater Thunderbird into an expensive, bloated four-seater sedan, triggering much ire and consternation from die-hard sports car enthusiasts, including those within Ford. The consensus was that McNamara's supremely uncompromising, numbers-driven approach didn't necessarily make a good car. He had no particular feeling for the various qualitative factors that separate a compelling automobile from a dreary one, and he resented any engineer, executive or sales manager who opposed those factors.[9] For example, a Ford engineer witnessed McNamara, who was head of Ford Division, walk into his first meeting waving a piece of paper. Only it wasn't a drawing of an inspiring car design as everyone had anticipated, but a list of numbers. He had jotted down a desired length, weight, cost, investment level and price with no consideration for how the car should look or feel.[10] On another occasion, in the early 1950s, Ford was struggling with how to fit freshly painted bodies into drying ovens that had been installed for the Model T. They were too small for the large automobiles that had come into vogue. The penny-pinching McNamara, then corporate controller, suggested that Ford cars be built in two pieces and then painted and welded together. One of Ford's manufacturing executives flatly told him the idea was preposterous. A chassis could not be welded together after the body was painted without severely weakening the structure. When McNamara persisted, the man snapped: 'The problem with you is that you don't know a goddamn thing about how our cars are actually made.' McNamara banned the executive from further meetings on the subject.[11]

To his credit, many of McNamara's ideas were ahead of their time. He was one of the earliest advocates for automotive safety and was absorbed with the idea of incorporating greater fuel efficiency and even emissions control when most people didn't even know what that meant. McNamara tenaciously fought for safety standards, such as seat belts anchored to steel plates, a padded instrument panel and padded sun visors, rearview mirrors that could absorb head impact should a driver or passenger strike it, strong door locks, deep-dish steering wheels and front and back seat supports to reduce the possibility of them being projected forward in a crash.[12] He argued that the number of injuries resulting from auto accidents could be cut in half, but these innovative ideas contravened the rules: when changes didn't appeal to car buyers, they didn't resonate with car manufacturers. In 1956 Chevrolet outsold Ford by

Robert McNamara.
(National Automotive
History Collection,
Detroit Public Library)

a margin of 190,000 units. Henry Ford II grew impatient, finally griping to a reporter, 'McNamara is selling safety, but Chevrolet is selling cars.'[13] With hindsight, had Ford shown more confidence in McNamara's foresight, the company would have competed more successfully against the impending (though unforeseen) onslaught of well-built, low-priced small Asian cars, powered by economic engines.

## The Ford Falcon

Asian and foreign cars were becoming increasingly popular in the US, and the Ford Motor Company desperately needed to counter such an invasion. In 1959, Ford placed all its hope on McNamara's pet project: the no-frills, cheap (a modest $1,912), stubby, extremely bland but reliable 1960 Ford Falcon series (1960–70), which was remarkably economic. It was the smallest car Ford had sold in the US since 1930. Though the company had played with the idea of compact car designs for years, the idea of small cars was dismissed when the economics didn't match with the public demand; their reasoning was that it would cost almost as much to build a small car as it would a standard model, only to attract a limited market. Although Henry Ford II approved McNamara's development program for a new small car, the mood in the industry insisted that compact cars would never be profitable in America. McNamara's judicious attitude was that building a bigger car where a smaller one would do was wasteful and waste was something McNamara could not abide.

Despite the Falcon's mundane appearance (it was about as exciting as a twelve-pack of RC Cola), it had excellent performance (30 miles per gallon), and that endeared it to the budget-conscious public, resulting in stratospheric sales of 417,000 units in its debut year – an unprecedented achievement, accounting for 25 per cent of Ford's total volume and proving the critics wrong. There's no accounting for taste, though, as some insiders wondered if the results would have been greater had the Falcon not been such a doormat. Among the critics was the company's thirty-six-year-old marketing manager, Lido 'Lee' Iacocca. Ford now frantically needed another car with mass appeal to get into the black. The company, though relieved by the success, was still looking for a miracle and, relying on a shoestring budget, was acutely aware of the brevity of the situation. The clock was ticking.

Although the Falcon was a hit, it failed to meet McNamara's ambitious sales projections of more than 600,000 units. The Falcon never came close to this figure and never would. Nonetheless, if Ford had continued in the same

1964 Ford Falcon. (National Automotive History Collection, Detroit Public Library)

direction as the Falcon, it would have been a greater adversary to the later invasion of Asian imports. Had McNamara remained with Ford, he might have tried to analyse that shortfall, but his time with the company was nearly at an end. What resulted from the introduction and success of the Falcon was an internal conflict between two different philosophies of management represented by two opposing titans: the impetuous Lee Iacocca and the uncompromising Robert McNamara. McNamara was a virtuoso, orchestrating common sense, a Bauhaus architect, while Iacocca was the barbarian at the gate, dreaming in skyscrapers to the tune of Wagner's 'Ride of the Valkyries'. Though there was acrimony between the two, they held each other in high regard. McNamara was the archetypal incorruptible public servant, whose intelligence Iacooca viewed as formidable, but which obscured his true gentle and shy character.

McNamara was named the company's president on 9 November 1960, at the age of forty-four. He was the first non-member of the Ford family to hold the position but only did so for thirty-four days; no sooner had he been promoted than he left for Camelot, accepting President-elect John F. Kennedy's offer to make him Secretary of Defense (a role he continued to hold in Lyndon B. Johnson's cabinet). Like someone with too much testosterone, McNamara couldn't pull out of the Vietnam War, which became ignominiously known as 'McNamara's War'.[14] Many at Ford weren't sorry to see him go. His critics, of whom there were many, said he had no real sense of the cars and trucks the company built, nor did he relate to the company's culture. Fifty-six years after leaving Ford Motor Company, McNamara still symbolises the great divide in the auto industry between 'bean counters' and 'car guys', a chasm that McNamara may be personally responsible for. Lee Iacocca, who replaced Jim Wright as general manager of Ford Division around the same time, had no illusions about why the Falcon had missed its mark. Iacocca had in some respects been McNamara's protégé, but his perspective was very different from that of his former boss because Iacocca was something McNamara had never been: a salesman.

# 3

# ENTER IACOCCA

When McNamara left Ford, the thirty-seven-year-old Iacocca was promoted as vice president and general manager. He realised that the Falcon had obvious flaws and its success was merely a result of its affordability. Consequently, the Falcon was not a big profit-maker regardless of its sales. To keep the price down, McNamara ignored extra-cost options or high-end models. Iacocca could be arrogant and sometimes brusque, but he was a far more political animal than McNamara and was fluent in the messy, unscientific emotional machinations of the selling process that McNamara disdained.[15] Where Iacocca really outshone McNamara, and many other Ford executives of the time, was in his savvy grasp of the market and the customer.

Lee Iacocca. (National Automotive History Collection, Detroit Public Library)

## The Fairlane Committee

Lee Iacocca had for some time said how limited recent Ford products were in scope. Immediately after his promotion in November 1960, Iacocca was determined to improve Ford's conservative image. To achieve such an ambition, he was shrewd enough to know that stimulating emotion would be the key to success, such as with a sportier new car. Selling the concept to Henry Ford II, however, still reeling from the 1958–60 Edsel catastrophe, would be a monumental challenge, so to convince Ford's president, Iacocca needed to gather conclusive data for a persuasive argument. Discreetly, he assembled a group of Young Turks from different departments. On appearance, the group appeared like middle-class, clean-shaven, straight-laced individuals, but behind the buttoned-up façade was a group eager to express its creativity. The first Kennedy administration was in place and it seemed as though anything was possible. 'We were young and cocky,' Iacocca later recalled. 'We saw ourselves as artists, about to produce the finest masterpieces the world had ever known.'[16]

The group consisted of product planners Donald Frey, Hal Sperlich (who would join Iacocca at Chrysler years later) and Donald Peterson; marketing man Bob Eggert and Frank Zimmerman (he had joined Ford at the same time as Iacocca and they developed a close friendship during their training program days); copywriter Sid Olsen (from Ford's advertising agency, J. Walter Thompson); marketing manager Chase Morsey Jr; advertising manager John Bowers (also from JWT); public relations manager Walt Murphy; and Ford racing director Jacque Passino. Notice that there were no accountants on the team. Iacocca viewed accountants as lacking imagination and he had had enough of the prudent and judicious McNamara era.[17] The group gathered each week for fourteen weeks at the Fairlane Motel in Dearborn, Michigan, for clandestine meetings. It was an opportunity to get familiar and talk privately while avoiding any ears in the walls and alerting Henry Ford II. Iacocca even burned all evidence, i.e. notes taken at the meetings.[18] The group became known as the Fairlane Committee and through their discussions Ford's future took shape – at least so they hoped. What is remarkable is that no one at Ford knew about the group and their intent to build a sports car, but it was too soon to approach the top brass with such a controversial concept. Iacocca kept the company busy with incremental steps.

First, Chevrolet was riding a wave with its two-seater Monza, a cosmetically altered version of its economic Corvair. Ford viewed the car with derision, scoffing at it as a dud, but it had a sporty appeal that made it successful. Ford, by contrast, had no similar equivalent. Iacocca quickly tried to salvage the Falcon's utilitarian image with some nip and tuck surgery. He set out to put vital oomph back into the Ford product line by installing a V-8 motor into the Falcon sport coupé, introduced a Falcon convertible and a two-door Falcon Futura with bucket seats and added fastback roofs to some of the larger Ford models, like the Galaxie, but these were mere indulgences. In his mind, Iacocca instinctively felt there was no better way to revive the company then to appeal to the youth market and the research from Chase Morsey Jr, Bob Eggert and marketing's Frank Zimmerman produced the material to back this claim. Iacocca predicted the emergence of the Baby Boomers (those born between 1945 and 1955), that they would become the significant factor as new car purchasers within five to ten years (claiming 40 per cent of the market share), including women. Furthermore, with the majority being college-educated, unlike in previous generations, it meant higher incomes. Though the market research seemed optimistic, indicating that this flourishing market was not made up of died-in-the-wool conservatives willing to accept outmoded fashions, Iacocca knew people were fickle and never trusted focus groups or market research. 'People don't know what they want,' he grumbled. 'Ya gotta have an idea and then ya gotta push it down their throats.'[19] Iacocca is reputed to have described the climate in 1961 as that of 'a market in search of a car'.[20]

Part of the dilemma in developing a 'sports car for the masses' was how to capitalise on the brand equity enjoyed by Ford's Thunderbird. Would the new model be a smaller, two-seated version of the T-Bird? Would the new car cut into the profits of the Falcon? The cost of development was a major consideration as well. At the time, the costs of building a new car exceeded $100 million and could rise to $400 million, a scenario that would be vetoed by Henry Ford II. Cost to the consumer was another issue. Special Projects Assistant Hal Sperlich came up with the solution – build the new car on the Falcon's already existing chassis, drivetrain and suspension to save both time and money.[21] The group recognised the public's desire for a low-cost sporty car and the T-5 Project was born. The concept car brought engineers and designers together to turn the findings of the Fairlane Committee into a car, though there were still debates whether the car should be a two- or four-seater, the consensus favouring a two-seater.

Second, there was talk of Ford developing the diminutive Cardinal from Ford of Germany for the streets of America, but Iacocca knew what sold in Europe didn't necessarily translate into sales in the US and convinced Ford's top echelon that the Cardinal would be another Edsel. After some deliberation, Ford agreed, relegating it to European-only distribution. This was just as well, as it generated millions of dollars' worth of sales over the next decade in Europe. For Iacocca, the cancellation confirmed Ford's support for his premonitions, his vision for the future and possibly his conviction for his new car.

And third, it was time that Ford returned to professional racing. Both Henry Ford II and McNamara thought racing was extravagant and unprofitable, but Iacocca knew that what was successful on the track was usually successful off the dealership floor. Even enrolling into racing was met with defiance from the American Manufacturers Association (AMA). Following the crashes into the grandstands at the 1955 Le Mans and in the 1957 NASCAR season, killing dozens of spectators, the AMA placed a ban on factory-supported racing. Consequently, the automotive industry essentially disappeared from NASCAR, though this did not stop Chevrolet, Chrysler and Pontiac from competing in stock car races. By pure luck, a Texan by the name of Carroll Shelby (a superb racer and winner of the 1959 Le Mans in an Aston Martin) approached Ford with the hope that the auto manufacturer would need a real sports car, or better, a racing car. The former chicken farmer had quit racing due to a heart condition and now concentrated on a career as a car designer based in Venice, Califiornia. He had heard that AC cars in England had lost its engine supplier and that Ford had a small-block V8. Shelby proposed a collaboration under his own brand, Cobra, incorporating Ford's 260 cubic inch V8 muscle into a lightweight British sports car, the AC Ace, replacing their Bristol straight-six (in the years to come, this would be modified from the 260 to the 289 and later replaced by the super heavyweight, the 427). When packaged together, these cars had enough venom to kill any competition. Shelby's motivation was to build great sport cars, not to sell cars. Jacque Passino jumped at the opportunity as a means of getting back into racing against the likes of Corvette, while simultaneously cementing a testing and development program under the umbrella concept of 'Powered by Ford'. The Ford Motor Company had just

Carroll Shelby. (National Automotive History Collection, Detroit Public Library)

Replica Shelby 1966 AC Cobra. (Clive Branson)

Shelby 1965 Ford Daytona coupé. (Clive Branson)

broken in a new engine, the Windsor 221 in. (3.6 litre) engine – a small-block V8. Though Shelby/Ford became a successful partnership, not enough Americans heard about the accomplishments on the tracks over in Britain and elsewhere in Europe and something closer to home would be indispensable.

Ford's racing drought ended in 1963 when American Formula One star Dan Gurney asked Lotus builder and Formula One team owner Colin Chapman to build a car to compete in the renowned Indianapolis 500 – the Mecca of American racing. Chapman agreed, providing Gurney could supply him with a powerful and durable enough engine that could withstand the taxing distance. With his lightweight and innovative designs, including a rear-engine formation, Chapman needed a 350 hp engine to beat the more powerful yet hefty Offenhauser-powered roadsters, which looked like massive iron lung machines on wheels. Gurney introduced Chapman to Ford and a deal was sealed. Ford offered an all-aluminium 256 cubic inch version of the Ford Fairlane's small-block V8. It was naturally aspirated, used four Weber carbs and was good for an estimated 375 horsepower on gasoline. The turbocharged four-cylinder Offenhauser engines, the standard engine at Indy, put out about 450 horsepower and ran on methanol. Ford's deficit, however, was made up through the Lotus 29's lightweight distribution and agility, especially it's speed through corners.

The Lotus became the first oval racing car to be equipped with a rear engine. Though Jim Clark didn't win his debut performance in 1963 (coming second, with Gurney coming in seventh), it didn't diminish Lotus's limelight. Clark went on to win the Milwaukee 100 in the Lotus 29's second race that year. By 1965, practically every team had converted to the rear-engine format as Clark raced to victory at the 'Brickyard' by an astounding 2 minutes, leading 190 of the 200 laps in a Lotus 38. He finished second the following year behind his compatriot Graham Hill (in a Ford-powered Lotus), and distinguished Ford as the manufacturer to beat, cementing a huge public relations coup. The ban ended when Ford announced that the company would again begin participating openly with their own Ford brands (and not just an engine supplier) in NASCAR and then in drag racing at NHRA venues.

## A Diversionary Tactic

A sports car theme still irked Iacocca. He liked the concept but was dubious about its selling potential. Furthermore, he wasn't pleased with the blueprint efforts he had seen circulating at Ford. He was in Gene Bordinat's design department when Bordinat presented him with an illustration of a wedged-shaped sports car – the T-5 – drawn by Phil Clark, a young designer with the design studio. As with the origin of the Mustang name, there are conflicting views as to who initially thought of the T-5 sports car. Some say the two-seater rose directly out of the Fairlane Committee and that Don Frey made the first sketch; others maintain it first appeared from the bowels of Bordinat's

Advanced Styling department. Bordinat boasted that the design was developed seven months prior to Iacooca ever seeing it. 'That car would have made it to the marketplace without Lee,' stated Bordinat emphatically.[22] Impressed by the style of the car, Iacocca ordered a clay mock-up version and once completed, he invited prominent racing drivers to view it. The car seemed so dynamic that racers Dan Gurney and Sterling Moss agreed to test-drive it at New York's venerated Watkins Glen track in front of a sold-out US Grand Prix audience in 1962. The reception for the car from the spectators and the press was ecstatic as it sliced through the circuit and along the straightaway, moving faster than air out of a whoopee-cushion, reaching an impressive 120 mph.

What was truly amazing was that there was no official go-ahead from Ford. The Fairlane Committee met discreetly at the motel at night and in a storage room by day, like Agents 86 and 13 in *Get Smart* meeting in a grandfather clock. 'The whole project was bootlegged,' Mr Frey told *USA Today* in 2004. 'There was no official approval of this thing. We had to do it on a shoestring.'[23] Though the T-5 or Mustang I had no connection with the final Mustang pony car, Iacocca was astute enough to use the T-5 as a gauge to test the waters in a publicity stunt and garner the public's reaction for a new sports car. The concept car was aimed to link Ford with high performance and it succeeded. It was also used as a device to encourage engineering students to consider careers with Ford. Bordinat assigned chief stylists Bob Maguire and Damon Woods to this project, with Maguire focusing on the exterior and Woods on the interior. Under them were executive stylists: John Najjar, a forty-three-year veteran at Ford who co-designed the Lincoln Futura, a concept car that served as a base for the Batmobile for the 1966 TV series *Batman*; Jim Sipple, to develop an innovative mid-engine sports car; and, of course, the twenty-seven-year-old stylist Philip T. Clark, whose designs were emblazoned with a galloping horse motif. Clark was later involved in the designs of the Ford GT40 and the Ford Cortina. Also included were engineers Herb Misch and Roy Lunn to help meet the sixty-day deadline.[24]

Bordinat's team drew up plans for a sports car with a centre-mounted V4 engine and four-speed transaxle, both borrowed from Ford of Germany's Taunus front-wheel-drive compact. The control arms at the corners were also of tubular steel and were suspended by coil-over shocks. The wheels were cast magnesium measuring 13 by 5 inches with disc brakes up front and drums at the rear. The 1.5-litre German V4 engine wasn't the fastest on track, only producing 90 horsepower, but it was nimble and could accelerate from 0 to 60 in 10 seconds thanks to its low, ground-hugging, all-independent suspension and lightweight frame totalling a mere 1,500 pounds, even when wet. The clutch was hydraulic and the shifter worked via cables. Both the steering wheel and foot-pedal assembly could be adjusted to fit the length of the driver; this was necessary because the leather-covered aluminium bucket seats remained immobile.[25] The car was furnished with colour-coded instruments sunk neatly into their individual circular consoles and an adjustable 3-inch steering wheel. The skin was stressed aluminium riveted to a multi-tubular steel chassis

Mustang I concept car. (National Automotive History Collection, Detroit Public Library)

constructed by California's Krutman & Barnes. Hidden headlamps and a hideaway licence plate, for weekend racing, were further innovative features.

It looked like an open toy car. The front was reminiscent of an angular Lotus Elan while the back was something straight from the pages of a 'Flash Gordon' comic strip. The roll bar wasn't even high enough to protect the driver's head, but the car could move like quicksilver. It stood just 40 inches high and stretched 186 inches at a cost of $2,500.

In an unprecedented move, the design for this low, sleek sports car went from drawing board to clay mock-up to actual performance in twenty-one days.

## The Emergence of the Mustang II

Though the peppy T-5 wowed spectators and press alike, Ford's accounting department wasn't so impressed, arguing that a two-seater sports car would produce insufficient numbers to justify the cost of production. So it was back to the drawing boards with the mandate for a four-seater, but time was at a premium.

Ford's styling department had now built seven different clay models; yet again, none of them seemed quite right with Iacocca. He realised he needed a car that gave the impression of a sports car, but a car that could be used by everyone, including the family. Then it occurred to him – develop a 'small-sporty' car.[26] Iacocca instigated an intramural design competition among Ford's three design studios: Donald Frey's Ford Division (Joe Oros, David Ash, Gale Halderman and John Foster), the Lincoln-Mercury Division and Gene Bordinat's Corporate Advanced Projects (Bob Maguire, Damon Woods, John Najjar, Jim Sipple and Philip Clark). The parameters were that the car had to weigh 2,500 pounds and be no more than 180 inches in length, with four seats, a floorshift and a decent-sized trunk, packaged at the reasonable cost of $2,500 with a host of options that would allow the buyer to customise the car to their individual tastes (meaning you could get all the perks from a vanity mirror to a supercharged engine).

# 4

# MUSTANG II

Don Frey was among the first at Ford to acknowledge that the Baby Boomer generation, which was starting to come of age, was a future target audience (by 1964, the first Baby Boomers would be eighteen years old and eligible to drive. Daddy could buy the car.). 'I realised we were sitting on a powder keg,' he said. 'Even if Iacocca claimed all of it, he deserved much of the credit. He had a major role in marketing, creating the whole mystique and the advertising campaign,' added Frey. "And he said to make [the Mustang] a four-seater, which was a key product decision. Up until that point, we had been thinking two-seaters. But he was right; there was a much bigger market for a four-seater.'[27] And if there was any one contribution that was key to the entire project, it was Iacocca's ability to pry loose the company purse strings to fund the thing. 'He took something like five shots with the senior officers of the company to convince them to put money into the car,' said Frey.[28]

In September 1962, the three studios rolled their concept vehicles out into the courtyard at Ford Design for Iacocca, Henry Ford II, Gene Bordinat and Don Frey to review. Of the six mock-ups presented, there were two cars that had potential: Ford Studio introduced the 'Stiletto', a gorgeous, Italian-styled combination of testosterone and exotic panache, but when management got a whiff of how exorbitant the projected cost of production would be, it was quickly axed.

The other car, designed by Dave Ash, had a short deck, long nose and a Ferrari-styled grille and was called a Cougar.[29] Henry Ford came down from his office twice to scrutinize the car. He squeezed himself into the back seat and barked that it needed more leg space. Henry Ford expressed his antipathy: 'I'm tired of hearing about this goddamn car. Can you sell the goddamn thing?' Iacocca assured him he could. 'But once I approve it, you've got to sell it, and it's your ass if you don't!'[30] This stern admonishment was as close as Iacocca was going to get to a stamp of approval from Ford, but the name had to go. The Mustang II was again introduced at Watkins Glen for the 1963 US Grand Prix and received the same enthusiastic response, though some were disappointed that it wasn't as sporty as the T-5/Mustang I. It now remained for the final design modifications to be incorporated into the initial production run.

Mustang II concept car. (National Automotive History Collection, Detroit Public Library)

## What's In a Name?

The team were still searching for the ideal brand name (a combination of 6,000 names, both from within the company and from their advertising agency, J. Walter Thompson, were considered) but Clark's horse icon struck a chord. John Najjar was a fan of the Second World War P-51 Mustang plane and is credited by Ford with suggesting the name (though this is highly contentious since there are a few who claim the credit). Company officials liked the name but thought the equine image was more suitable. The horse was dramatic and few symbols were so evocative of unleashed freedom. It personified the American spirit. Some Ford executives had reservations as to whether the stallion looked 'American' enough, so Clark, standing in front of them, simply added red, white and blue vertical lines behind the horse.[31] It was instantly accepted. Clark, who was right-handed, designed the horse galloping from left to right, facing anti-clockwise. A reporter mentioned to Iacocca that the horse was heading in the wrong direction, but as far as Iacocca was concerned, it was 'headed in the right direction'.[32] Clark's initial logo sketch was revised and finalised into a standard profile sculpture (with and without the colours behind it) by Charles Keresztes. Over time, the horse was modified to look crisper and more muscular.

Arjay Miller, the president of Ford Motor Company, was unequivocal that the new car could do well, but that it could also compromise sales of the Falcon. However, Henry Ford II liked Iacocca's presentation (his research data, engineering cost analysis and revolutionary car design concept) and that was the decision that mattered. Ford allowed $40 million to develop and tool up the Mustang. This would eventually be increased to $65 million.[33] The normal time allotted to manufacture a new car was three years, but Iacocca was given eighteen months to meet a 9 March 1964 deadline to get the car off the assembly line.[34] The advantage in Iacocca's corner was that most of the

Phil Clark's Mustang logo. (National Automotive History Collection, Detroit Public Library)

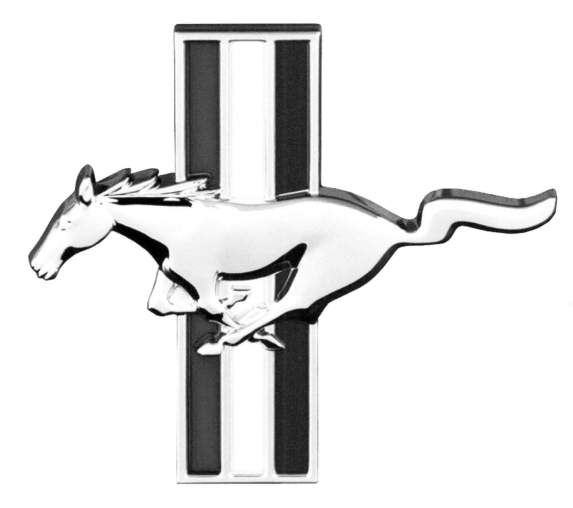

Charles Keresztes' Mustang logo. (Clive Branson)

Mustang's components would be from the existing Falcon platform. To give a sporty look, the new car's Falcon-based floor pan was dropped down around the engine/transmission, though the hood had to be re-moulded in order to accommodate the air cleaner and radiator.

To make sure the Mustang received undivided attention from the press and the public, Iacocca devised a plan to release the car at a time when he would not have to share the spotlight with any other car manufacturer and at a location where he could monopolise press coverage. He and Henry Ford II agreed that the launch pad would be New York World's Fair on 17 April 1964. This was a spotlight the world would see.

# 5

# The Launch Heard Around the World

Only a privileged few car brands have had a cultural impact on society. The Model T changed the face of America by indirectly developing middle-class suburbs and gave the public the opportunity to release themselves from the tentacles of confined transportation. It also introduced one of the greatest inventions, the assembly line. The Jaguar E-Type and Morris Mini became more than a means of transportation: they grew into cultural icons of the 1960s, an era centred on liberation. The E-Type and Mini encapsulated newfound independence from a rigid society, auguring an attitude of cultural, sexual and class rebellion. The Porsche 911 has been the embodiment of a brand setting the yardstick for all sports cars, having had the longest production run of any sports car. Few other automobiles in the world can look back on such continuity in technology, performance, design and longevity. And the humble VW Beetle. This disarming vehicle became the rallying cry for the underdog. With its air-cooled rear engine, spartan interior, hunched frame and an unmistakable sound, the Beetle replaced the Ford Model T as the most popular car ever made as it morphed into the counterculture for its unconventional yet reliable aura. However, like any product that achieves universal pop culture status, it became omnipresent as it took on multifarious national identities, affectionately known as the 'Bug,' the 'Kafer,' or the 'Fusca', but lost its original company's brand and control. Nevertheless, it's the phenomenal record-breaking sales (in its debut year) that the Mustang is renowned for as well as the social relevance and its historic longevity. A lot of this was attributed to the marketing, which touched a nerve in the American conscience. It didn't matter what age, sex, race or political affiliation you were, the Mustang seemed alluring to all. It became a talisman for youthful insouciance and resonated with the American penchant for freedom and idealism. Ford suddenly sold sex designed in metal.

## The Power of Marketing

Design can be viewed as the production of culture while marketing is the art of communication. Oliviero Toscani, one of the greatest advertising creative directors, stated to *Adweek*:

> The creativity of communication is conditioned by an obsessive search for consensus, in the false belief that consensus is success. Fear of failure always produces mediocrity, because the chosen solution will always be the least risky and the most banal. In most cases, doesn't even attempt to be original, but wants, rather, to be a mediocre and repetitious replica of it.[35]

This is uncanny considering J. Walter Thompson's advertising campaigns weren't anything exceptional, especially when you consider how unparalleled the Doyle Dane & Bernbach (DDB) ad campaigns were for the VW Beetle around the same time, brilliantly adapting reverse psychology. Ford's advertising achievement was through ubiquitous and cleverly controlled marketing strategies that elevated anticipation, galvanising a public frenzy that was almost like Beatlemania.

Ford was the first carmaker to consciously target and successfully tap into a specific generation.

Lee Iacocca made no secret of the fact that his goal was for his new car to beat the Falcon's first-year sales. Of course, the Mustang broke all sales records, transforming the car into the benchmark for Ford for the next forty years while launching Iacocca as the 'father of the Mustang' and the greatest automotive marketing genius of all time. Iacocca truly became a household name when his face was splashed concurrently on the covers of *Time* and *Newsweek* magazines during the release of the Mustang. Heralded as the second coming, his reputation as a saviour of one of America's largest companies was revered as though he was a new addition to Mount Rushmore. Iacocca surmised that such coverage led to possibly a further 100,000 Mustang sales.[36] Years later, Iacocca repeated a similar accomplishment with Chrysler in the 1980s, resurrecting that company with equal aplomb. At the height of his popularity, 90 per cent of the American public identified him. His recognition was greater than many politicians; and there was even talk of him possibly running for president in 1992. Philip Caldwell replaced the fired Iacocca in 1978 and replaced Henry Ford II as CEO and chairman of the board. Ironically, he is credited in being as successful as Iacocca in increasing Ford's profits by introducing the Ford Taurus and Sable, but was not as publicly recognised, probably because he lacked Iacocca's flair for the media's limelight. Caldwell retired in 1985. Both men are inductees into the Automotive Hall of Fame.

Ford elevated the Mustang's image in how it used advertising, both in cost and in effectiveness, by investing in one of the most expensive vehicle launches in American auto history: a $10 million advertising and marketing campaign[37] aimed at enticing the younger generation while courting the female sector with taglines such as 'Life was just one diaper after another until Sarah got her new Mustang' and 'Mustang has become the sweetheart of the Supermarket Set.'[38] Imagine the furore if a company used such condescending remarks today.

Four days prior to the Mustang's 17 April dealership launch, Ford initiated an all-out media blitz. Iacocca invited 125 prominent magazine journalists from publications ranging from *Car and Driver*, *Businessweek* and *Sports Illustrated* to *Look*, *Popular Science* and *Playboy* to Ford's pavilion at New York World's Fair for an exclusive presentation. The premise was to introduce the Mustang and stress the necessity of linking Ford with the emerging Baby Boomer market (72.5 million Americans). Later that day, the journalists were treated to the keys for a drive – a caravan of 150 Mustangs covering 750 miles from New York to Dearborn, Michigan. The sight of a 150-strong convoy of new Mustangs certainly turned heads and had tongues wagging. *Car Life*'s review gushed, 'It's a sports car, a gran turismo car, an economy car, a personnel car, a rally car, a sprint car, a race car, a suburban car and even a luxury car.'[39] One of the more unique highlights of the World's Fair was the opportunity for visitors to ride on a closed automated circuit at the Ford Pavilion in one of fourteen Mustang convertibles called the Magic Skyway.

The next day, 11,000 magazines and newspapers received Mustang press kits while 200 of the nation's top radio disc jockeys and college newspaper editors were given a sneak peek at the Mustang in Dearborn. The buzz was electric, as reflected by *Time*'s response:

> This week, Ford's new Mustang sports car, one of the most heralded and attention-drawing cars in autodom's history, drives into showrooms all over the U.S. In it rides a big bundle of Ford's future and the reputation of the man who daily test-drives a different Mustang between Bloomfield Hills and Dearborn. The man is Lido Anthony Iacocca, general manager of Ford's Ford Division.[40]

But it was *Car Life*'s editor Dennis Shattuck who phrased it best when he coined the new Mustang model as a 'pony car'.[41] The moniker has remained to this day, describing a 'sporty' coupé moulded with a long hood and a short trunk and powered by a V8 engine.

On 16 April, on the eve of the official dealership launch, Ford bought parallel TV commercial slots for all three primetime programming between 9:30 and 10 p.m. An ad in *TV Guide* teased, 'The most exciting thing on TV tonight will be a commercial.'[42] During a commercial break from the sitcom *Hazel*, 29 million Americans were suddenly exposed to galloping horses, good-looking women and the vastness of the open, rugged terrain with the promise of something unexpected and exciting for tomorrow – a prophetic statement. The adverts were like defibrillators to revive a complacent population.

Full-page newspaper and magazine double-page spreads in 2,600 major publications, including twenty-four national magazines, showcased Mustang advertisements.[43] The ads had minimal copy, just an inducement: 'The Unexpected.'

An ingenious and remarkable stunt was to locate small car owners across the nation and mail them Mustang advertising flyers. Mustangs were also displayed like starlets in 200 Holiday Inn lobbies and at fifteen of the nation's top airports. No feat was too big nor too challenging as Ford went to great heights in New York City for a photo opportunity at the top of the Empire State Building. To

Ford Mustang print ad. (National Automotive History Collection, Detroit Public Library)

make it possible, a Mustang convertible was disassembled so the pieces would fit into the elevators, then reassembled on the 102nd floor's observation deck.[44]

As an unexpected bonus, Walter Hoving, chairman of the prestigious jewellers Tiffany & Company, presented Henry Ford II with the Tiffany Gold Medal for Excellence in American Design. The Ford Mustang was the first automobile to receive such an exalted honour. To add to the suspense, all Ford dealerships were ordered to keep their quota of Mustangs under wraps, away from public view. Some salesmen even had Mustangs concealed in their own garages.[45] As the media hype reached a crescendo, the unveiling of Ford's new 'Pony Car' on 17 April 1964 caused near pandemonium, with over 4 million people converging on Ford showrooms across America during the first week.[46] Salesmen in dealerships were accosted by crowds acting almost like rabid autograph hounds. More than 22,000 cars were ordered on the first day.[47] Dealers were overwhelmed with the response and needed to revert to their 'Mustang Order Holding' form that helped them to close sales when the dealerships had been stripped of any remaining Mustangs.[48] Bidding wars and actual fights broke out between potential customers. One buyer slept in his Mustang in the showroom until his cheque was cleared the next day.[49] In some cases, dealerships had to close their doors. Overnight the Mustang became the most popular car ever, selling 418,812 units by its first anniversary and

3 million in its first decade. Iacocca explained that part of the tremendous success was to get the car to the market before any competition:

> An ambitious goal would be about 18 months pencil-to-market, an unheard of short time span. I recognized the New York's World Fair was about 18 months away, and it would be a great venue to introduce the car with intrinsic free advertising. I felt if I introduced this new car line mid-model year as a 1964½ model, I would have the advantage of introducing a new car to a captive audience without any distractions from all other new-car manufacturers who typically introduced their new models in the fall.[50]

In May, Ford capitalised on the Mustang's popularity by securing the bid to be the Official Pace Car for the 1964 Indianapolis 500. Ford presented three Mustangs modified by Ford's NASCAR racing shop Holman-Moody to be equipped with 289 High Performance (HiPo) engines and suitable supporting brakes and suspension to reach the mandatory 140 mph pace speed. The pace car was driven by Henry Ford II's grandson, Benson Ford, driving in front

1964 Mustang coupé. (Clive Branson)

of more than 300,000 spectators and seen by millions of TV viewers. In addition, Ford presented another thirty-five convertibles as VIP cars to escort the forty-eighth running of the Indy 500 Festival Queens for a one-lap salute (they were later given to race dignitaries). The winner of the race, A. J. Foyt, received as part of his victory package a free Mustang. It is reported that he gave it to his maid.[51] Consequently, Ford produced 185 spin-off Pace Car replicas in hardtop for the buying public, complemented with a similar racing livery and paint job (the Indy car's hue was slightly off the standard Mustang Wimbledon White), and equipped with a milder 260 V8 instead of the 289 V8 HiPo conversion. The assigned 1964 Indy Pace Car convertibles are considered by collectors to be the rarest Mustangs of all.

The Mustang's success was built on the following:

- It met a growing demand for a small, affordable and economic automobile (for its time). The car's price tag closely equalled its weight at $2,300 for a base six-cylinder hardtop with three-speed stick (many of its contemporaries started their price tags at $3,000). A significant number of buyers were persuaded to spend a further $1,000 on high-profit options like the 289 V8, automatic, console, power steering and brakes, styled steel wheels, and vinyl top. There were also 'special' highfalutin' packages, such as the GT Equipment Group and the Décor Interior Group, to ensure your Doris Day version could become Raquel Welch, and the Special Handling Package that equipped the car with quicker steering and stiffer springs, shocks and sway bar and red 'Hot Wheel' brand tires. Iacocca's marketing genius worked to the tune of $1.1 billion in net Mustang profits for Ford;
- It had more options than a greasy-food parlour menu;
- To keep production within a tight budget, the Mustang was built almost entirely off the bones of the compact and inexpensive Ford Falcon. Designers gave it a distinctive surgical styling that appealed to a wide demographic audience as a sporty economic trendsetter. Its distinctive long hood and short trunk gave the impression of a powerful engine housed underneath, a novel design that spawned an entirely new breed of vehicle from the stable – the Pony Car;
- And finally, Iacocca promoted the hell out of it. The car was cleverly advertised mid-year to avoid competition and seized global attention by launching it at the new World's Fair. It also didn't hurt to spend millions of dollars marketing the car simultaneously in magazines, newspapers, exhibits and TV commercials. Such mass exposure was the advantage of having limited, but highly concentrated, media access.

The result of this strategy blew the doors off the anticipated sales figure of 100,000 by reaching an unequivocal sales record, eclipsing the Falcon's staggering record of 417,000 by a mere 1,638 units (and sales of the combined 1964 and 1965 units topping 686,000. Today, the auto market is too fragmented for a single model to monopolise such staggering numbers in one year). With such insatiable public enthusiasm, Ford needed more production space for Mustang units and transferred the production of the Ford Fairlane from both its Dearborn and San Jose plants to the Kansas City plant in mid-June while adding the Mustang to Falcon and Comet production at their Metuchen, New Jersey plant in February 1965.[52] By the summer of 1964, over 160,000 cars had been produced to meet dealership orders. The Mustang's awe-inspiring success secured Iacocca's future as an important part of Ford's enclave and it would seem his promotion to the top job as president was imminent. Or so he thought…

# 6

# 1964–1965: Setting the Benchmark

Ford Mustang production was hampered by a UAW strike, leading to shortages of parts. To make up time, the assembly was restarted five months before the normal start of the 1965 production year. As a result, the early production versions are often referred to as 1964½ models, but for the record, Ford management never referred to the original car this way. Mustangs built between March 1964 and August 1964 (using a generator) were VIN-coded (car's identification) and titled 'early 1965' models while those built after August 1964 (using an alternator) were called 'late 1965' models.[53]

What was displayed on the small screen wasn't entirely reflected on the showroom floor. Instead, the Mustang was modestly rigged out with a three-speed floor-shift transmission fitted to a standard, budget-conscious Falcon 170 cubic inch, inline six-cylinder engine and cost a bit less than its 2,572 pounds in weight at around $2,400.

It was dressed with the usual incentives: three-prong spoke wheel covers, padded dashboard, carpeting (poorly fitted) and aluminium-outlined bucket seats which were literally sealed in place and couldn't be adjusted. You couldn't order the GT Equipment Group because it didn't exist. And forget the 289 High Performance V8 – it was only supplied to the Ford Fairlane. The door handles were clip-ons, the hood seemed to have a hair lip (this was corrected later on), and the biggest gaff of all, due to the hastiness of production, a limited number still had the horn ring bearing the Ford Falcon logo unconvincingly covered by a trim ring with a Ford Mustang logo. These characteristics made enough difference to warrant designation of the 121,538 early versions. Of course, these salient points didn't endear Ford to the automotive press as the skewers emerged: piercing, burning comments about the lack of handling, stability and power. Fortunately for Ford, the American public showed its infatuation with the car as much as with the myth.

With time, the six-cylinder/three-speed that achieved fame with the budget-conscious consumer began to fade and was usurped by the steroid-induced V8 powerplant. By 1971, the six-cylinder was only housed in 10.8 per cent of Mustangs. Ford continued its tradition of inflating what was once light and sporty, diverting Iacocca's original strategy of a pony

1965 Mustang coupé. (Clive Branson)

car into a bigger, heavier and more expensive touring sedan by 1966. The 'muscle car' phase was spearheaded by the popular Pontiac GTO and Ford didn't want to be the bridesmaid. In June 1964, Ford added the much-needed bellow of a 289 High Performance V8 to the Mustang arsenal along with the necessary supportive ammunition of a mandatory four-speed, 9-inch rear end, heavy-duty suspension, upgraded camshafts, a dual-point distributor, a 595-cfm four-barrel carburettor, header-style exhaust manifolds, larger rod bolts, screw-in rocker arm studs, and an open-element air cleaner. Overall it produced 271 hp at 6,000 rpm.

It was hardly serendipitous that a Mustang convertible should appear in the latest James Bond film, *Goldfinger*, driven by Bond's equally curvaceous female companion. Ford realised how successful the Bond series was and wanted to capitalise on its popularity. Such foresight was confirmed by the *Guinness Book of World Records*, which listed *Goldfinger* as the fastest grossing film of all time.

By September, a more aggressive-looking Mustang joined the line-up to compete against the Corvette and the Jaguar E-Type. Initially, Ford only

1965 Mustang fastback. (Clive Branson)

wanted to offer the public two body styles – the hardtop and the convertible – but the company also needed to fill the void for the new Total Performance slot – an all-out assault on every form of motor sports to generate sales, and this meant the production of a racy model with its own distinct trappings. Gale Halderman, who drew the original Mustang shape, had the answer with his drawing of a wind-swept, aerodynamic Fastback 2+2 (initially drawn in 1962).

## 1965: The Shelby Influence

The Total Performance had three purposes: first, to garner exposure and sales for the Mustang and Ford through various racing genres; second, to help increase technical and mechanical development by testing on circuits; and third, Henry Ford's personal vendetta against Enzo Ferrari. In 1964 Ferrari was in dire financial straits and Ford was willing to buy out Ferrari, negotiating a deal for $16 million. Stipulated in the contract was that Ford would acquire all aspects of Ferrari's company, including its racing program. Upon hearing the translation of the contract, Enzo Ferrari vehemently refused and terminated the deal. This incensed Henry Ford II and he vowed to get even with such a snub by beating Enzo at his own game – at Le Mans, the marathon 24-hour endurance race that Ferrari had dominated since 1960. In collaboration with Carroll Shelby's design team and Ford's in-house designers, Ford spent millions in development for a car that could outperform Ferrari, but failed to even finish the race each year. It was a humiliation until 1966, when a modified version of the Ford GT40 was unveiled. Ferrari heard about the improved GT40 and upgraded its cars accordingly, but during the gruelling race, each of its cars expired while Ford took first, second and third. Ford was the first American car manufacturer to win the most prestigious auto race and confirmed its legendary status by winning it the next four years. Ferrari has never won since.

*Get Smart*, *Sonny & Cher*, *Hogan's Heroes*, *Star Trek* and *I Dream of Jeannie* all premiered on the small screen while 'Like A Rolling Stone', 'Satisfaction' and 'Yesterday' debuted on the radio. The Vietnam War was now an armchair war for millions of Americans to watch on TV each night, only to be interrupted by a news bulletin that Malcolm X had been assassinated in New York City or coverage of the Watts riots in Los Angeles. Sandy Koufax pitched his fourth no-hitter, and Craig Breedlove broke the land speed record at 600 mph. It was the end of an era marked by the death of Winston Churchill, yet the US auto industry had its biggest year ever, with production, sales, employment

1965 Mustang fastback. (Clive Branson)

and profits soaring to all-time highs. It was 1965 and the 'muscle car' craze – its aura and reputation overshadowing automakers' mainstream models – moved from back page articles to a testosterone-percolating movement. The power and speed that ruled the professional circuit now spilled out into the concrete jungle. Ford's mandate was two-fold. First, Ford was determined to reclaim its mastery in professional racing. To Iacocca and his colleagues, the principle was 'race on Sunday, sell on Monday'. Whether it was drag racing, TransAm, SCCA or endurance racing, Ford desired to become synonymous with it and ultimately in the Winner's Circle. Second, the basic Mustang was by no means a true muscle car, but it wasn't wallpaper either and with a bit of tweaking, it had the adaptability to become a contender in the right hands. The car had to have obvious brawn and enough sex appeal to have men, while looking at it, walk into lampposts or talk in monosyllables. Basically, Ford supplied the bare-bones 2+2 from its San Jose plant in California and Shelby-American gave it the meat and muscle.

## Drag Racing

Ford entered drag racing with their recent Fastbacks carrying a monstrous 427 big-block SOHC V8 Cammer/C-6 automatic combo, winning the NHRA Winternationals (A/FX class) in 1965 with Bill Lawton behind the wheel of a Tasca Ford Mustang that could deliver 650 horsepower (this would be increased to 1,000 horsepower the following year). His nickname became Mr Factory Stock Eliminator. Fellow Mustang competitor Gas Ronda won the NHRA Top Stock World Championship the same year. The 427 SOHC would be the last factory-sponsored foray into drag racing until the Cobra Jet-engine Mustangs debuted in 1968.[54] As the sport grew in popularity, fierce battles for Funny Car supremacy erupted with names that became legendary: Don 'The Snake' Prudomme, Tom 'The Mongoose' McEwan, Raymond 'Blue Max' Beadle, Sox & Martin, Ed 'Revellution' McCuloch, Larry 'Hawaiian' Reyes, Jim 'Jungle Jim' Liberman and Mickey Thompson, who led Ford's challenge.

## SCCA/Trans-Am Racing

Ford was tired of having sand kicked in its face by General Motors' Corvettes in the Sports Car Club of America's (SCCA) B Production class. Ford needed Mustang to degrade them as impotent beach muscle boys. To do so, it needed to inject some serious steroids into Halderman's design. Ford, having seen the success Carroll Shelby's Cobra sports cars achieved, approached Shelby with an offer he couldn't refuse. In August of 1964, armed with several Mustang Fastbacks, Ford wanted the Shelby-American team in Venice, California, to midwife a high-performance Mustang for street and track to win the respectability it thought it warranted. Of course, this didn't come without some internal grumbling. As far as Ford's Performance Department was concerned, Iacocca giving the assignment to Shelby-American – an outsider – was a piece of sleight-of-hand tantamount to treason. As a result, Shelby-American was on its own, and many from Ford hoped it would fail, but that didn't faze Carroll Shelby. He seemed to thrive on controversy.[55]

## The GT350

Stamp collecting would never replace the excitement this beast offered. This is a vehicle the Car Gods must have designed just to put the cat among the pigeons. As a street car it's about as practical as a used-up lighter, but who cares? This is one of those dream machines that strikes you as hard as the first time you were spanked as a child. This is a top predator on the food chain, equipped with the power, agility and aesthetics of a tiger. If people thought the Mustang was harmless, they were sorely mistaken. Shelby transformed the innocuous pony into a thoroughbred by creating the retina-thrashing GT350 (and the GT350R for racing), renaming the series Mustang Cobra, apparently from a dream he had. Shelby told *Mustang Monthly* that:

> A plane-load of people came from Detroit trying to decide what to call it. And after the third meeting, I said, 'A name doesn't make a car, a car makes a name.' So we're sitting around and I said to one of our guys, 'How far is it to that building over there?' He said, 'What the hell you talking about?' And I said, 'Step it off.' He came back and reported, 'It's 348 paces.' I said, 'We're going to call it the GT350.'[56]

The car was revealed to the public on 27 January 1965, the same month that Shelby-American moved its production facility from its humble quarters to its larger facility. Apparently the average warehouse wasn't big enough, so they moved to a facility that could house a 747 at the Los Angeles International Airport. At the stratospheric cost of $4,547 (the median middle-class salary was just under $7,000), the GT350 was the first race-ready car ever to be marketed by an American auto manufacturer.[57] The GT350s were sold through dealers who also handled Shelby Cobras or directly through Shelby's factory at an added cost of under $2,000.

The GT350 street version underwent an immediate diet, shedding 200 pounds by replacing the steel hood with a fiberglass replica, removing the back seats, placing the battery into the trunk (though this caused intoxicating fumes to enter the car and the battery was later returned to the engine compartment). Additional changes were the Cobra valve covers and a hi-rise intake manifold, Glasspak side-exhaust pipes, a functional hood-mounted air scoop, five-cluster instrument panel, stabilizer, 15-inch wheels with magnesium Cragar rims, Kelsey Hayes ventilated discs in front and heavy-duty metallic-lined drums

1965 GT350. (National Automotive History Collection, Detroit Public Library)

in back with equally modified Koni spring suspension. It was dressed in the customary Wimbledon White with the Guardsman Blue racing stripes (though the majority remained completely white) and wore the racing striped rocker panels touting the GT350 name. Best of all, it was saddled with a K-Code 289 cid V8 Hi-Po engine, four-speed manual transmission that exuded 35 horses more than the standard 289 cid version, elevating it from 271 hp to 306 hp. It was fast and cornered and handled superbly, but wasn't designed to be practical or family-friendly. It was also noisy and about as comfortable as filling out a tax form, but it had a stentorian roar that sounded like it emerged from Hell. *Road & Track* punched out on their typewriters their admiration about the GT350's acceleration (0 to 60 in 5.2 seconds, pushing brain matter to the back of the cranium), 'You simply feed on enough throttle to break the tires loose, feather it slightly to pick up traction, then mash on it and watch the tach needle wind around toward the 6,500-rpm red line.'[58]

Shelby-American built sixty-six fewer units than was required by SCCA but 516 street units were manufactured to compensate. Ford dominated the series

1965 GT350. (Clive Branson)

with the driving skills of Jerry Titus, Ken Miles and the incomparable Mark Donohue claiming the cherished National Championship. Mustang repeated the feat in '66 and '67 as well as winning the '66 Manufacturers' Championship in the inaugural SCCA Trans-Am series, and again the following year. Ford never had sand kicked in its face by Corvette again and converted the publicity accolades into handsome sales. Shelby later confessed to *Mustang Monthly* in 1990 that the GT350 was his favourite Mustang, preferring the 289 to the 427. 'It's a no compromise car built to get the job done.'[59] The GT350 was a disguised racing car for the city tarmac. Shelby had the capacity to produce 2,900 models in 1965–66, but orders were backed up for five months by the end of the run. Hagerty Insurance estimates the value of an original GT350R at between $700,000 and $1 million. In all, 562 Shelby GT350s were produced in 1965, making this a car highly sought after by collectors. Of those, thirty-six GT350R models were built exclusively for road racing.

# 7

# 1966: The Record Breaker

While Shelby-American built the speciality GT series, Ford continued with the regular Mustang brand. Some purists believe the Shelby Mustang improved with age, while others argue that the once-unique original Mustang became foreign and lost sight of its role as an 'everybody's car'. Regardless, they couldn't argue that 1966 wasn't a monumental year for the Mustang, breaking all preconceived expectations with a record landslide of 607,568 sales for a single year (this is a combination of Ford and Shelby-American sales), a criterion that has yet to be broken by the Mustang or any other car brand. Though there were marginal changes between the '65 Mustang and the '66 version, Ford ventured into new directions by developing modified and 'special' Mustangs, such as the GT series. This approach has become de rigueur to this day.

On 23 February 1966, a white Mustang convertible rolled off the Dearborn assembly line as the millionth Mustang built, confirming Ford's pony car to be the fastest to reach seven digits. To celebrate the auspicious milestone, a 'Limited Edition' Mustang was built for the occasion. The Limited Edition Mustang lapsed back to a six-cylinder engine with a decal denoting its place in history. Other modest additions were equipped with exclusive wire wheel covers with distinctive stripes and accented rocker models. It was the shortage of V8 engines at this time (Ford was out of stock due to the high demand) that accounted for what enthusiasts felt was an anti-climactic tribute to such an auspicious triumph.

## 1966 Mustang Convertible

Ford eliminated the crosshairs across the honeycomb grille to give the illusion that the horse and corral were free-floating, creating an unobtrusive, sexier identity. A slight variation to the scallop side trim and a restyled gas cap completed the minor exterior upgrades. On the interior, the instrument panel was given a racier look by separating five gauges independently with their own in-depth, conical shapes, replacing the ordinary panel design borrowed

1966 Mustang convertible. (Clive Branson)

from the Ford Falcon. In addition, the glove box door was redesigned and the standard vinyl seat had an embodied 'woven' pattern. The engine was also the same as for 1965, continuing with the 289 2V and 4V engines.

Things only change when they affect enough people and it was reported by the United States Department of Transportation that the nationwide death toll in 1966 was 50,894, an increase of 6.84 per cent from the previous year, or approximately 1,000 road deaths per week.[60] Consequently, safety became a priority as 1966 was an unparalleled year for safety requirements that car manufacturers had to abide by, including front and rear seatbelts, a padded instrument panel, a collapsible steering column, safety door latches, dual brakes, standard bumper heights, rear window defoggers, non-rupturing fuel tanks and pipes (remember the Pinto?), emergency flashes, electronic wipers (they were vacuum-operated before) and windshield washers. Ford continued the profitable business of optional packages whereby customers could customise their cars. Although the coupé outsold the convertible, the ragtop was still a hot contender, selling more than 70,000 units. It was only $50 cheaper than the fastback, so it was hardly surprising that it outsold the fastback by a margin of 3:1.

## 1966 Mustang Coupé

The true measure of a car is in how clearly it interprets the desires of the public. It could be said that the 1966 Mustang coupé was the major factor in the Mustang's greatest success, becoming the best-selling Mustang of all time. The 1966 coupé still holds the record based on the 500,000 sales figure, legitimizing the 'pony car' market (Iacocca spearheaded Ford's profits through Mustang to the tune of $1.1 billion).[61] Despite the high production numbers, the coupé remains one of the most sought-after models for collectors, restorers and enthusiasts. The refinements made in '66, although subtle, gave the car a more classic façade. Nevertheless, 1966 would see the end of the small pony cars in favour of the burgeoning (and, by comparison, burlesque) muscle cars that were the dictates of American ardour. And while Mustang was to continue to be very popular on the American car scene, the brand would not enjoy such a scale of overwhelming success.

1966 Mustang coupé. (Clive Branson)

## 1966 Mustang Fastback

As 1966 progressed, all V-8/four-speed models received the Ford-designed Top Loader transmission. A 289 High Performance V-8 became available with the C4 Cruise-O-Matic; however, it would be the last production year for the original Mustang fastback due to a decline in sales of nearly 50 per cent, though the remaining 35,000 fastbacks are highly collectable today. This decline in popularity is rather ironic considering how the fastback style became a perennial favourite mould for muscle car styling, like the Dodge Charger, the Oldsmobile 442, the Mercury Cyclone, the Pontiac GTO Judge, the AMC AMX and the Buick GSX. Ford felt compelled to use the fastback style again with their muscle brands, Talladega and Torino. Based on accessory purchases, 71 per cent of customers ordered a V8 engine; 80 per cent wanted radios and white-walled tires; 50 per cent received automatic transmission; and one in ten Mustangs were sold with a rally pack.

## 1966 Shelby GT350

The 1966 model dropped the word Mustang from its name completely and some people speculated that the GT series was more Shelby than Mustang. In '65 the car was adorned with a racing pedigree: fog lamps, five-cluster instrument panel, wood grain sports steering wheel, front wheel disc brakes, stabiliser, flared trumpet exhausts, and a 289 cu. in. engine. The 350GT is a poorly camouflaged street-legal racing car. Its 271 was replaced by the hefty 289 V8 with 306 horsepower, accompanied by a four-speed manual transmission, heavy-duty suspension, larger wheels and tires, a fibreglass hood, functional quarter-panel air scoops that fed cool air directly to the rear brakes, twin racing stripes, new louvres on the rear window pillar with Plexiglass windows replacing the air vents, a Cobra tachometer and the installation of a folding back seat. The first 262 cars of the 1966 Shelby GT350 model production were actually leftovers from 1965. Changes for the second model year had to conform to stricter safety regulations, including the lowering of the front suspension and simplifying the under-ride traction bars. All the Cobra add-on goodies were still available for those who had Castrol in their veins and a clubfoot. The Cobra GT350 logo was tattooed onto the gas cap and colour choices were extended to include Candy Apple Red, Sapphire Blue, Ivy Green and Raven Black.

## 1966 Shelby GT350 Convertible

Only six 1966 Shelby 350GT convertibles were made and none were sold to the public. Carroll Shelby made them as tokens of appreciation for business associates and incentives for hard-working employees of Shelby-American. Each convertible was painted in a different hue and equipped with an automatic transmission. Because they are exceedingly rare, you can imagine the demand for them from collectors.

## 1966 Shelby GT350R

Stripped of any superfluous weight, the GT350R was a 100 per cent racing brute. Gone were the headliners, carpeting, upholstery, side glass and rear window (plastic was used instead) and only one bucket seat. A four-point roll cage, sheet aluminium inner door panels and fibreglass hood and roof. A 34-gallon fuel container replaced the regular 16-gallon fuel tank and standard gas cap. The HiPo 289 was taken apart while all the components were reassembled to new and precise specs, maintained by a buttress of heavy-duty brakes and shocks. Of course, all this came at a price at a staggering $6,000. This may explain why only thirty-four were built for the public, but its sole intention was to win on the track, not on the streets. It didn't take long to prove its mettle as driver Ken Miles piloted one to victory in its first SCCA outing in Texas. Shelby Mustangs won the B Production Championship in 1965, 1966 and 1967. How do you eclipse that?

## GT350H: Go With Hertz

Ford dealers complained that the company could sell additional Shelby Mustangs if the cars were made more consumer-friendly and comfortable, such as by including a back seat and offering more colour options. Shelby-American's sales director, Peyton Cramer, had the bright idea of approaching a rental car company to increase sales and Hertz took the bait when the car designers delivered a seductive GT350 in black and gold livery (only 200 were produced in this colour combination; the remaining 800 were in white with gold racing stripes).[62] Not only did Hertz agree to a deal, but the company eventually ordered 1,000 units. The cars were packaged as GT350H ('H' for Hertz) and affectionately known as 'Rent-A-Racer'. The sound it made was something akin to a large, wild and predatory jungle animal.

The GT350H models housed the normally aspirated 289 cu. in. Hi-Po engine that was reputed to have kept Ford among the top echelon in international racing. The engine had enough stamina to offer 306 hp at 6,000 rpm, producing 329 lb ft of torque. Without realising it, for a mere $17 a day, Hertz was offering a dream for anyone with hot blood and an itch for speed. In fact, Hertz was inundated with first-time renters and indirectly helped Ford nearly double Shelby sales. However to Hertz's chagrin, many of the rented GT350Hs returned in damaged condition from drag races or, worse, in some cases, the prized engine had been removed by some enterprising individuals and switched with the inferior 289 V8. Exasperated, and in an attempt to tame the volatile beast, Hertz halted production after the first eighty-five cars and ordered automatics instead of the four-speed manuals. Including the Hertz series, only 2,380 Shelby GTs were produced in 1966.

# 8

# 1967: A Fat Pig!

Lee Iacocca wanted to see cars as safe, simple and economical. If it required sex appeal, then in his opinion, give it sensuality not nipple rings and tattoos. So it is no surprise that he was not impressed by the changes that had evolved from the original Mustang. 'It's no longer a sleek horse,' wrote Lee Iacocca in his autobiography, 'it was more like a fat pig!'[63] He resented how the original concept of the sporty Mustang was dissolving into a hulking muscle car but, to be fair, the Mustang needed to adapt to comply with the public's demand for power. Since the advent of the 'pony car,' it was inevitable that competing auto manufacturers would catch up. By the mid to late 1960s, Chevrolet's Camaro, Pontiac's Firebird, Plymouth's Barracuda, AMC's Javelin and even the Mustang's corporate cousin, the Mercury Cougar, were strutting the boulevards, eating away at the Mustang's monopoly. And though the Mustang was more affordable, it was also showing its age in performance. To counterattack, Ford beefed up its stable, restyling its line-up for 1967–68 by stretching, pulling and adding a lot more calories thanks to a menu that consisted of a 390 cu. in. 6.4L V8, 320 hp big block engine. The 390 was a sound engine: not too feeble like the 289 or 302, but not overbearing like the 427. *Car & Driver* gave it the thumbs up:

> The idea of stuffing the 390 engine into a car originally designed for an engine less than half that size is pretty wild, and it leaves the way clear for some even hairier engines in the future. The 390 block is the same one used for Mercury's 410 and Ford's 427 racing engine and the 428 street engine. The bare bones of the '67 Mustang are plenty strong enough to take over 400 horsepower, so a measly 320 hp aren't going to bend a thing.[64]

It provided for ordinary citizens an excellent drive: fun to drive, well-built, good handling and braking, comfortable and inexpensive. *Road & Track*'s reaction, however, wasn't exactly complimentary: 'The 1967 facelift has retained all the identifying characteristics of the first series but has fattened up the Mustang in all directions. It still has that chunky look about it and frankly, looks a bit old-fashioned beside its new competitors.'[65] Ford tried to make the car more aerodynamic by giving it a ground-hugging effect and adding 2 inches in length and 2.5 inches in width.

1967 Mustang fastback. (Clive Branson)

1967 Mustang fastback. (Clive Branson)

To compound problems, the automobile industry had a rough year in 1967 with most of the blame falling on the shoulders of labour problems. Ford was crushed by a forty-nine-day strike, putting its earnings loss in the third quarter at approximately $74 million — an absolutely staggering amount of money in 1967. The UAW union agreement with Ford, Chrysler and GM provided wage boosts of nearly a dollar per hour for workers, forcing the price tags of American cars to increase and allowing cheaper foreign imports to set a new sales record with 785,000 sold. Overall, Mustang sales lagged behind their 1966 record, with no help from production costs and wages, an increase in insurance rates, safety and environmental enforcements, and even the American involvement in the Vietnam War, which literally pulled hundreds of thousands of young men out of the market. Nevertheless, though the competition was making an indent into the Mustang's profits, Mustangs still managed to outsell their nearest American competitor, the Chevrolet Camaro RS, by a ratio of 2:1 with reported sales of 71,042 fastback Mustangs, 44,808 convertibles and 356,271 coupés that year: a total of 472,121 units off the dealership floors.

## 1967 Mustang Coupé

Though the '67 coupé appeared to be just a slightly larger version of the original, its compact size gave it a greater swagger that was absent in the original model. The front grille retained the galloping horse with its corral

1967 Mustang fastback (back). (Clive Branson)

surround, but the enlarged opening gave the car more presence. The scallop side scoops, though non-functional, were designed as two smaller scoops with inlets, replacing the chrome version with a more seamless look in identical colour to the body. The back swept cleanly to a concave rear panel with recessed rear lights. All of these features contributed to a more uncluttered, more aerodynamic look and Mustang finally divorced itself from its Falcon roots for a fresh all-Mustang interior.

## 1967 2+2 Fastback

As they slipped the covers off its body during its inaugural car show, heads must have turned, mouths dropped, people walked into each other and conversations probably halted in mid-sentence. This was not your typical tool of transportation. Its slippery sleekness looked like it had arrived from another planet – a shape that only the wind could mould. And when the ignition was turned on, its rumble was closer to something that would emerge from a garage at Sebring, Daytona or Spa Francochamps. The fastback actually looked healthier on a much heftier diet, from its extended, streamlined roof that stretched back like a yawn to the concave rear tail. The car had spunk, with separate triple tail-lamps, a longer snout and bigger grille, a ribbed rear panel instead of the chrome bezels, and hooded dual recesses.

1967 Mustang collection. (National Automotive History Collection, Detroit Public Library)

## 1967 Mustang Specials

Ford zeroed in on particular regional 'soft' spots in promoting Mustangs, such as Los Angeles and Denver, which were lucrative markets for Mustangs, accounting for over 20 per cent of sales. Trying to be as appealing as dopamine, Ford introduced a limited edition 1968 GT/CS, otherwise known as the 'California Special' and the 'High Country Special.' Production was limited to fewer than 5,000 to breed a sense of exclusivity to Southern California and Colorado dealerships. The only differences to this model were superficial cosmetic additions such as an emblem-free, black-out grille with rectangular fog lamps; decorative side scoops; special side striping; indigenous scripts; a built-in rear spoiler; sequential taillights; and vernal coloured schemes of Timberline Green, Columbine Blue and Aspen Gold. Flattery will get your everywhere.

## 1967 Shelby GT350

Not every customer wanted to race, so Ford forced Shelby-American to tone down the GT350 (this would remain a contentious point between Ford and Shelby). Though Shelby-American tried to soften the edges, the car remained bulletproof with a Cobra Paxton Racing engine. To Shelby, changing its integrity was as unthinkable as giving up his first born. Ford's accounting department got jittery and saw the Cobra as a little rough for its market audience and that it didn't level well regarding return of investment. They viewed it as a low-volume, low-profit, and high-expenditure enterprise. Ford informed Shelby to make it like other Fords for the purpose of profit. In other words, all the fun parts were made redundant or optional. Ford's insistence caused a divisive reaction from Shelby, whose uncompromising attitude felt the suffocation of Ford's managerial myopia. He didn't like to pander to anyone, including the hand that fed him. 'Big corporations tend to destroy the cars they create,' he told *Mustang Monthly* in 1990. 'All of the corporate vultures jumped on the thing and that's when it started going to hell.'[66] The words came out like a bad taste in the mouth. The Mustang maintained record sales but reached uninspiring designs towards the second generation and remained so until the late 1990s when, ironically, the car returned to what Shelby had originally proposed: something with attitude and muscle. Although some other pony and muscle cars have seen a revival, the Mustang is the only original pony car to remain in perpetuity over five decades of development and revision.

As Ford expanded its muscle-clad Mustang with room for a 390-cid big-block testosterone, Carroll Shelby went one better by stuffing in a hulking 428 for his new GT500. Modifications culminated in the development of power through a hemi-vortex, dual carb, centrifugal glands with a quad intake for an upgraded throttle response. And that was just to power the door lock. The adrenalin-pumped performance took the race replica concept to an entirely new street level.

## 1967 Shelby GT500 and the Emergence of the Mighty Cobra

This is a car you should be required to take a driving test to operate. Its power is almost uncontrollable. The steering was equivalent to arm-wrestling a Second World War landing craft. The GT500 was introduced in 1966, but it now housed the big-block Cobra Le Mans 428 cu. in. V8 pumping out 355 hp, based on the 427 cu. in. V8 that had swept the top three places at Le Mans. The '67 model also came with a few aesthetic alterations. It was the first car to adapt a racing roll bar across the top of the cabin. The trunk lid, combined with the tail end, formed a wind-cheating ducktail, and the rear-quarter windows were replaced with rear-facing air scoops.

But the new, nose-heavy 428-powered GT500 wasn't what Carroll originally envisioned. By then, he was ready to pack it in. When interviewed by *Mustang Monthly* in 1990, he confessed:

> I was committed because Lee [Iacocca] wanted me to build the GTs, which I helped out with, but it just went from bad to worse politically. I'm not knocking Ford, because when you get into bed with a big company, they're all the same. I started trying to get out of the deal in 1967 and it took me until 1970 to get production shut down.[67]

Ford took advantage of the excessiveness behind Shelby-American's design because it had the desired effect in selling more Mustangs, but the company

1967 GT500. (National Automotive History Collection, Detroit Public Library)

also felt that its control was losing grip: even the name Mustang was being sacrificed for Shelby or Cobra. The last straw was when the Shelby Mustangs featured central headlights and B-pillar red marker lights inside the air extractor scoops. These immediately raised the ire of law enforcement as vehicle code violations and, months later, Ford took Shelby Mustang manufacturing away from Carroll and brought it back to Michigan, where it could regulate tighter scrutiny. In 1967, more GT500s were sold than GT350s. That year's model set the precedent for future GT500s, although it was the last Mustang of the era to have Shelby's idiosyncratic touch.

## Shelby GT500 Super Snake

Shelby's GT500 'Super Snake' recently sold at the Mecum Auctions in Kissimmee, Florida, for a staggering $2.2 million in 2019 – the most expensive Mustang sold at auction. You may ask yourself, 'What is a Super Snake?' It was a one-of-a-kind prototype requested by Goodyear Tires as a high-speed test vehicle for its new line of tyre, the Thunderbolt. Shelby complied and with his chief engineer, Fred Goodell, at the helm he instructed his technicians to install a 427 cu. in. racing V8 engine, producing 650 hp. The engine was race-prepared for the application, bolstered with weight-saving aluminium heads and pistons, a single-car intake, a 7,000-rpm kit featuring exceptionally light valves and crank, and feeding this bully with a 780-cfm Holley four-barrel, complemented by a specifically designed oil cooler. A four-speed and Detroit Locker 4.11 rear axle completed the package. The only difference between its outside and the regular GT500 was the triple narrow-wide-narrow Guardsman Blue Le Mans stripes. But the rest was pure ogre.

   The test took place at Goodyear's 5-mile oval track in San Angelo, Texas. Journalists from *Time* and *Life* magazine accompanied staff to witness Fred Goodell establish a new record by averaging 142 mph for 500 miles. And to top it off, Carroll Shelby drove journalists around the course, topping 150 mph. The test was a complete success with the Thunderbolt tyres retaining 97 per cent of their original tread and the car exceeding 170 mph. When the car was shipped back to Shelby-American's facility, Shelby planned on building fifty more to sell through Shelby dealerships until Ford learned of the price of $7,500 – twice that of a normal GT500 – and promptly shelved the project. Although Shelby-American built two other 427-powered 1967 GT500s, the Goodyear test car would go down in Shelby history as the only 1967 GT500 Super Snake. Of course it probably helped its value that millions of viewers noticed a replica version of it in the 2001 blockbuster *Gone in Sixty Seconds*. But that trick had been done before. In 1968 it was far more successful.

# 9

# 1968: Bite the Bullitt and Brute Force

In 1968, auto manufacturers implemented a controversial price-cutting measure: shortening warranties. Until then, most warranties had been 24,000 miles or twenty-four months, but this year the standard warranty was reduced to 12,000 miles or twelve months. The warranty covering the powertrain remained covered by a five-year or 50,000 mile warranty. To add insult to injury, Ford increased their price tags on all their models. What you received in return (for the basic models) was new heated rear windows, self-adjusting anti-skid brake systems and mandatory headrests. But what was truly astonishing happened behind closed doors. In February, Henry Ford II unexpectedly hired Semon 'Bunkie' Knudsen, chief executive at General Motors, as president of Ford instead of the man who made the Mustang a household name and saved the company. This caused ripples among the assembly lines of America. Though shocking, it wasn't entirely surprising. Ford was losing its grip on the muscle scene and Knudsen was reputed to be the perfect antidote with his record for GM's performance vehicles. Knudsen was tailor-made to be GM's president. He had a master's degree, served with GM for twenty-nine years, reversed the downward spiral at Pontiac and set sales records at Chevrolet, yet GM choose Ed Cole instead.

One reason Knudsen may have accepted his new role with Ford was possibly to get even with General Motors and beat its star pupils, the Corvette and the Camaro. Iacocca recalls from his autobiography, 'Henry was a great GM admirer. For him, Knudsen was a gift from heaven. Perhaps he believed Knudsen had all that famous GM wisdom locked in his genes.'[68] Suspicion soon became derision between Knudsen and Iacocca. The atmosphere was filled with backstabbing and subterfuge. Iacocca was about to quit but he knew he had a great deal of internal support and he was out to make life difficult for Knudsen. Needless to say, Knudsen had a vision backed by Henry Ford. Unfortunately for Knudsen, he was never fully able to push his agenda because of too many insuperable obstacles and too much opposition.[69] The whole thing came off like a Judas handshake.

Three months later, Knudsen hired Chevrolet's most talented designer, Larry Shinoda (designer of the exotic 1963 Corvette Sting Ray and the understated

'67 Camaro Z-28), as head of the Special Projects Design office. Together, both were adamant in giving the pony car some much-needed machismo. Knudsen was determined to introduce a new generation of Mustangs that would be sleeker, faster and bolder. He kept his word and eventually produced the Mach 1, the Boss 302 and the Boss 429. Though these models had enormous power, their size and ungainliness lost what made the original Mustang so popular. Ford envisioned the next generation of Mustangs (the same way it had interpreted its sporty Thunderbird) from a pony car to a luxury vehicle, possibly a sedan, with softer suspension, a roomier interior and a quieter ride. The obsession to appeal to the gearheads seemed to blind Knudsen to the looming insurance restrictions, costs and tighter emission regulations, not to mention the greatest threat: the oil embargo. This would take hold of America in the early 1970s and force auto manufacturers to rethink their roles. Lee Iacocca was an advocate in preventing the direction Ford and Knudsen were heading in. 'If we hadn't gone nuts and put the big Boss 429 in, the car never would have grown in size,' he said later. 'That was what triggered it out of the small-car world – performance, performance, performance.'[70]

Knudsen had an aggressive drive, almost compulsive, for high performance and couldn't (or possibly wouldn't) adopt any other approach.

1968 Mustang Fastback. (Clive Branson)

Fortunately for Iacocca, Bunkie's tenure was short-lived: it was a mere nineteen months before he was fired. He discovered why people don't leave one auto company for another. Often it's cultural and the victim is the one who usually offends. Henry Ford II and Iacocca's relationship remained caustic, but at least Ford begrudgingly accepted his second-in-command as the new president. Iacocca recollects from his autobiography about Bunkie's fall from grace. 'I wish I could say Bunkie got fired because he ruined the Mustang or because his ideas were all wrong. But the actual reason was because he used to walk into Henry's office without knocking.'[71] As for Bunkie himself, in 1971 he went on to become chairman of White Motor Corporation, a maker of heavy-duty trucks and agricultural and construction vehicles. He pulled the company from a dire financial state to profitability in eight years. How effective was Knudsen? After he retired from White Motors in 1980 the company soon went bankrupt. Knudsen died eight years later in a Detroit area hospital at the age of eighty-five. But not everything was acrimonious for Ford in 1968. Two great things happened: first, a movie; and second, the release of the most powerful Mustang to date.

## Bullitt

It is remarkable how a movie can make a statement that becomes etched into a nation's psyche, be it a character, device or vehicle. One such film is *Bullitt*, made in 1968 by Peter Yates and starring Steve McQueen as Frank Bullitt, a hard-nosed police lieutenant. Our protagonist drives a modified '68 Ford Mustang GT 390 Fastback through the streets of San Francisco and this, intentionally or not, became a metaphor reflecting America in the 1960s as a sexy, confident and uncompromising nation. The image of this Mustang (the sound, the look, the aggressiveness) captivated audiences. The combination of style and a famous 10-minute chase scene immortalised the car and catapulted the Mustang, as an American icon, to near legendary status. Film critic Emanuel Levy wrote in 2003 that, '*Bullitt* contains one of the most exciting car chases in film history, a sequence that revolutionized Hollywood's standards.'[72]

The Ford Mustang is so closely associated with the film that in 2008 Ford released a second *Bullitt* edition, the Ford Mustang GT, for the film's fortieth anniversary. This was a closer facsimile of the original film's Mustang. A third version is planned for 2019. Based on reports from Wikipedia, the last remaining Charger and one of the two Mustangs were scrapped after filming because of damage and liability concerns, while the other was sold to an employee of Warner Brothers. The car changed hands several times, with McQueen at one point making an unsuccessful bid to buy it in late 1977. The car is currently owned by Sean Kiernan in Tennessee; his father bought the car for $6,000 in 1974 after responding to a listing in *Road & Track*.

1968 Mustang Fastback. (Clive Branson)

The car remains one of the most sought-after models for serious car collectors and pony car enthusiasts. The other Mustang, a stunt Mustang, was found in 2016 at a junkyard in Mexico and was officially verified by an automobile authentication expert.

## GT500KR: King of the Road

By 1967, the GT500 housed a 428 V8, essentially a more suitable performance version of the 427 FE for the streets, but it wasn't until 1968 that a brand-new birth of the 428 (7 litre) Police Interceptor V8 engine came, with improved heads and larger exhaust manifolds. What emerged was the 428 Cobra Jet engine and it was baptised the GT500KR. This is a car that must have been designed by God on glue. Hammer the throttle and leave today in yesterday. The KR insignia stood, rightfully so, for King of the Road. To prevent reducing sales due to rapidly escalating insurance surcharges, the output was 'officially' rated at 335 horsepower, but according to independent tests, the actual output was 410 horsepower, more credible given the engine's 440 pound/ft of torque, capable of accelerating from 0 to 60 in under 7 seconds, mind-blowing numbers for 1968. Of course, with such overwhelming brawn, the DNA needed to be strengthened. A first-time Shelby RAM-air was introduced. The functional hood scoop allowed more air to be sucked in by a vacuum-activated butterfly valve that funnelled the air directly into the 735-cfm Holley four-barrel. The immediate boost was a rush of 410 bhp. Everything was standardised for performance: power front discs, braced shock towers, a beefy 9-inch rear end, staggered rear shocks (on four-speed models), and an 8,000-rpm tach as a required accessory for all four-speeds. Part of the deal was the inclusion of the GT Equipment Group so the customer was assured of having a healthy helping of extra-large of everything: heavy-duty suspension, F40 tyres, fog lamps, chromed quad exhaust tips and GT identification. The GT should have stood for Good Times.

The sound of the streets in 1968 was the screeching of burnt rubber. The Shelby GT500KR Cobra Jet could be construed as the Eighth Wonder. The KR sealed its place in history as the most powerful Mustang ever built (as of 1968) and a remarkable measure of success in the collaboration between Ford and Shelby-American. According to various sources, the KR monogram was established before the car was even designed. Allegedly, Carroll Shelby got wind that Chevrolet was planning on trademarking the same title for a new Corvette, so he called his lawyer to trademark it immediately (threatening

1968 Mustang GT500KR. (Clive Branson)

1968 Mustang 429 engine. (Clive Branson)

that otherwise he would find another lawyer that same afternoon) and beat Chevrolet to the punch, much to the competition's chagrin.[73]

But there was another exceptional player involved, a Rhode Island Ford dealer by the name of Robert F. Tasca. He used his initiative to build his own colossal engines and proved their mettle on the drag strip. Tasca merged elements from existing 390, 427 and 428 FE-series V8s to develop a stock pony car capable of clocking a quarter-mile in 11 seconds at 120 mph. The top echelon in Detroit noticed and listened. So when Tasca came calling, the door was wide open. Following Tasca's lead, Ford installed a 428 passenger-car block as a base, adding 427 low-riser heads with an aluminium Police Interceptor intake with a big 735-cfm carburettor. The engine was packaged for the coupé, fastback and convertible. 'The Cobra Jet began the era of Ford's supremacy in performance,' carped Tasca. 'It was the fastest, in my opinion, production car built in the world at that point.'[74] And just to emphasise the point, any doubts were dismissed when a Cobra Jet Mustang, driven by Al Joniec, took top Super Stock honours by breaking every 1968 NHRA record and walked away with the Winternationals title. Ford couldn't pay for better public relations. Though Tasca's advice might have been an embarrassment to Ford's engineers, it was also a game-saver. Ford appreciated Tasca's involvement so much that it offered him three opportunities to permanently join the Ford Motor Company, but he declined for family reasons and to stick with his family dealership business. To his credit, he agreed to put his business acumen and vast experience to further effect, allowing his Mustang dealership to be used as a training centre to help instruct other Ford dealers worldwide. He travelled extensively throughout North America and Europe, giving lectures and workshops on quality service. In 1971, he switched, at Iacocca's request, transferring from Fords to Lincolns and Mercurys. By 1986, Tasca Lincoln-Mercury was the world's leading L-M dealership.[75]

Even when stationary, the street version gurgles like someone using mouthwash and snorts to life, emitting a giant burst of sound that causes dogs to flee. At the time, *Car Life* magazine said, 'The car is so impressive, so intimidating to challengers, that there are no challengers.'[76] What makes this car rare is that the GT500KR only had a three-month production run (from May to July). Feeling the constraints from government to conform to emission and safety regulations, the Ford Motor Company dropped the GT500KR after '68, right before Carroll Shelby stopped modifying Mustangs, ending production at a little over 1,200 units. Today, the KR is regarded as the ultimate Shelby Mustang produced and is among the most expensive muscle cars when it hits the auction block, having been known to command over a six-figure asking price.

1968 Mustang GT500KR. (Clive Branson)

An amusing side note intended to bring about greater GT500KR sales was an internal promo that was marketed entitled 'The 1968 Summer Sales Program'. The top salesmen would be rewarded with all expenses paid trips to *Playboy* resorts in Wisconsin or Jamaica while the top dealerships would receive promotional visits from *Playboy*'s elite Playmates. The Playmates attracted hundreds of potential buyers to gawk in dealerships across the United States and Canada. Lee Marvin, James Garner, Paul Newman, Kevin Costner and Bruce Willis are noted celebrities to have owned a GT500KR. Though 1968 wasn't a stellar year for Ford Mustangs, ironically it was the most successful year in the history of Shelby Mustang, the credit attributed to the immensely popular Cobra Jet engine, which continued to be available until the end of 1970.

1968 saw a prodigious amount of models: the Mustang 289 coupé, the GT fastback, the 2+2 fastback, the GT428 fastback with the Cobra Jet engine, the 302 hardtop, the six-cylinder hardtop, the GT390 fastback, the GT428, the GT500, the Shelby GT350, the Shelby GT500KR, the Shelby GT500KR convertible, the Shelby GT500 with the 429 engine, and the Special Edition California coupé. Ford allowed consumers to custom-design their own specifications, so your regular Mustang coupé could look like a GT, with GT crest and accessories, without actually being one.

A modified 1968 Mustang GT350. (Clive Branson)

The standard 1968 Mustang, in comparison to the GT series, was about as exciting as gel moving in a lava lamp. Nevertheless, despite increased competition and marginal cosmetic changes from the previous year, the Mustang coupé remained supreme in its field as the hottest selling pony car. Hardtop sales were just shy of a quarter-million in 1968. Its 200-cid, 3.3L straight six may not have been impressive on paper, but with an intentionally lighter load, stripped of 300 pounds of excessive weight, the coupé could challenge any comparable muscle while being more economical. The front grille bars had disappeared, the twin scallop scoops were replaced with a simple one-piece chrome unit, and for the first time script-style lettering was used instead of block letters on the side trim. A GT Trim Package attire consisted of F70-14 tyres mounted on GT-styled steel wheels with a vented look as trim rings, hood vents, a GT emblem, and fog lights were back while new shoulder belts were enforced by safety regulations. What set the '68 model apart from the '67 was under the hood. The familiar 289 V8 was replaced with the new 302 V8 (this engine would remain with Mustang for the next twenty years while the K-Code Hi-Po V8 was officially retired from production. It is so rare it has become somewhat of a Holy Grail among collectors). Capable of 390 hp, the 427 V8 seemed infallible, reaching 60 mph in 6 seconds. The fastback version had a choice of engines that was like comparing a greyhound to a pit bull: a 302 or a mammoth 428.

The dominance of a 428 Cobra Jet as an optional engine (based on the 428 Police Interceptor for the GT Equipment Group) under the belt of a fastback or hardtop meant the speed to give performance enthusiasts goose-bumps by clocking a quarter-mile in just 11.62 seconds. Everything on the 2,253 Cobra Jet fastbacks and 564 hardtops had been reinforced, including shock towers, RAM-Air induction, suspension shock absorbers, four-speed manual or six-speed automatic. All are highly sought-after by collectors.

If Gran Turismo (GT) was stapled on the side of your car, people would pay attention, particular to the baritone emitted by either a 427-cid or a 428-cid 7-litre mean machine. As culture needs decadence, progress needs barbarians, and the GT provided both. These GT packages broke all language barriers and remained top on the bestseller list for performance-oriented Mustang buyers. This was heaven on wheels, furnished by disc brakes that could stop spit in mid-air and married to heavy-duty suspension. Together, it reached a crescendo at its ignition. A new C-shaped graphic was introduced to articulate the sassy side scoop, GT emblems were tattooed on the side panel, and to ensure the racy pedigree, there was a pop-up chrome fuel cap that definitely made a pony car look like a muscle contender dripping with body oil.

The small-block GT350 4.9L 302-cid might not have been running for Mr Universe (the standard 350 offered 250 hp compared to the former 289), especially against the Camaro Z-28, but it could be supercharged up to 6,400 rpm, as Carroll Shelby did with the GT500. Shelby's prototype 428 could

A modified 1968 Mustang GT350. (Clive Branson)

belligerently flex its muscles at any challenger with its rear tires spinning at 80 mph, yet it never entered a dealership. The GT350 was certainly more controllable with power steering and brakes, claiming 355 hp at 5,400 rpm and 420 lb/ft at 3,200 rpm. This was no slouch, torching the length of almost four football fields in 6.5 seconds. The race for street muscle supremacy became a marketer's haven. Ironically, the GT350 remained the performance choice for road and street racers while the GT500 was gentrified as Grand Touring.

# 10

# 1969: A Steed for Every Need

An amorphous-shaped piece of metal can be curved into a sculptured piece of art and the Mustang had expanded into a gallery of magnificent mobile examples: convertible, hardtop (coupé) and SportsRoof (a rather pedestrian name for the tired fastback), as well as the new Mach 1, Grandé and, by mid-model year, the Boss 302 and 429 V8s. In addition, Mustang hit an all-time high of eleven optional engines from the standard six-cylinder to the colossal 428 Cobra Jet big-block. The offspring were the 428 Cobra Jet Q version that delivered a flat-front deck lid without RAM-Air induction; the 428 Cobra Jet R with a functional 'Shaker' hood scoop that protruded through a chiselled hole in the car's hood, channelling the air flow directly

1969 Mustang convertible. (Clive Branson)

to the engine's air cleaner for better combustion; and to make sure there was a Mustang for everyone, a Mustang E (for economy), utilising a standard SportsRoof mould and controlled by a six-cylinder engine with a low axle ratio and automatic transmission with a torque converter. When purchasing a 1969 Mustang, the GT Options Group was no longer required (for a Cobra Jet), though its output remained the same as the previous year at 335 horsepower. Also, the RAM-Air, which was previously included, no longer applied.

## The Mustang Hardtop

By 1969, the Mustang had matured into the ultimate American 'sporting' car. Gone were the pronounced side scallops, though dual headlamps and the extra pair of lights set into the outer area of the grille were a nice touch. The ever-present horse had escaped from its usual corral in the centre of the grille and galloped off-centre as a sole horse in front of its tri-colours. The simplistic minimalism, devoid of any superfluous fuss, gave an understated yet compelling look of confidence. The '69 models were stretched and lowered

1969 Mustang hardtop. (Clive Branson)

1969 Mustang coupé. (Clive Branson)

even further. They featured a shopping list of slightly altered modifications: dual horizontal headlights, a matte black, injection-moulded plastic 'egg-crate' grille design, a wider 'C' pillar and a more conventional roofline, parking lights recessed into an air slot in the front splash panel, and fewer vents for an overall seamless flow. Slip inside and face a double-hooded instrument panel for both driver and passenger, padded energy-absorbing arm rests (for when you were stuck in a traffic jam), nylon carpeting and encapsulated by an all-vinyl interior. Basically, the same inducements applied to the convertible except for a larger rear window.

## The Mustang Fastback (Sportsroof)

Just under half the Mustangs sold in 1969 were fastbacks, now named SportsRoof. What made it different from the hardtop and convertible was an even lower stance (by half an inch), a windshield rake increased by 2.2 degrees, an enlarged front grille housing four round headlights for the first time, a rear ducktail spoiler, simulated interior woodgrain for a feigned rural image and the ever present exterior side scoops for the exterior. Engine-wise, you had the same options as the hardtop.

## The Mustang Grandé

In an attempt to reach the world of exclusivity with its men's club interior and show-us-to-the-polo-club coachwork, Mustang introduced the Grandé, which was easily comfortable in the midst of Mercury Cougars, Camaros, Firebirds and the like and would be just as at home around country estates as it would be parked in front of a four-star hotel downtown. Designed to transport not the secretary but the oenophile, the Grandé offered satin-sheet inducements: wire wheel covers, dual colour-keyed mirrors, a two-toned paint stripe, wheelwell rocker panels, rear deck moldings and Grandé script lettering on the G-pillars. The most obvious difference in the Deluxe Decore Group was the added insulation, 50 extra pounds of heavy sound-deadening pads shoved under the carpets like a mattress. And to guarantee extra silk performance, rubber-cushioned mounts to eliminate any metal-to-metal contact between the rear springs and the axle and absorb unpleasant bumps. To ensure performance with luxury, the Grandé Package offered the option of any Ford engine. Surprisingly, the price of all this was under $3,000.

## The Cobra Jet

The 428 Cobra Jet was certainly a crowd pleaser because it was powerful enough to spit out a lick of flame from the mouth of its chromium-armoured exhausts. So it is of little wonder that this continued in most Mustangs through 1967–70 (even if it was sold as an option). But even this mega-powerplant

1969 Mustang Boss 302. (Clive Branson)

would be replaced in 1971 by the all-conquering 429 Cobra Jet based on Ford's new 385-series big-block. With canted-valve heads, the 429 Cobra Jet produced 370 hp, which was further upped to 375 as a Super Cobra Jet. Is there no limit? This came with the usual solid-lifter camshaft and the Holley four-barrel as part of the Drag Pack option. The only thing the Cobra Jet didn't have was a white contrail.

## The Mach 1 'Speed of Sound'

The fourth new Mustang for 1969 was a passport: a passport for speed called Mach 1, an appropriate name that replaced the snivelling GT as Mustang's muscle leader (only 5,396 '69 GTs were built and as a result it would be thirteen years before the GT saw the light of day again with Mustang.) Every inch of the Mach 1 looked like it was desperate to be unleashed: spoilers, stripes and scoops. This was a car that could blow out like a shotgun and blast through ravelled ribbons of road, though its preference was a straight line. It was the first Knudsen/Shinoda collaboration for Ford, and like everything they touched, it set the tone for speed and performance.

1969 Mustang Mach 1. (Clive Branson)

Regardless of what Iacocca thought, muscle was king of the street (and the circuit). Underneath the menacing matte-black hood was a 351 cid V8, a small-block engine with 250 horsepower standard and, if you still felt deprived, there was a 290 horsepower alternative. There was a cavernous bay area to fit the goliath 428 cid big-block with the option of the 335 hp Cobra Jet V8, with or without RAM-Air transmission, that had a sling-shot time of a quarter-mile in less than 14 seconds. More than 80 per cent of all 1969 Mustangs sold were equipped with V8 engines.

The roof was lowered with a more expressive rear spoiler, side scoops derived from the Ford GT40 race car, unique reflective stripes and Goodyear Polyglas GT tyres with sexy embossed white lettering. It was suited with NASCAR-inspired hood latches that reinforced the racer's edge. This was a hard-boiled sweet in a candy store with a simulated hood scoop, racing mirrors (an industry first), dual exhausts and a grille with the width and look of the mouth of a whale shark. It came with a Competition Suspension package that provided heavier springs and shocks and a larger sway bar. According to *Car Life* magazine's road testers, the '69 Cobra Jet Mach 1 was 'the quickest standard passenger car through the quarter-mile we've ever tested'.[77] Just under 300,000 units sold. To most auto manufacturers, these seemed like impressive numbers, but it was 17,000 fewer than in 1968, and worse, sales continued to slide for Mustang as competition crept ever closer.

## The Boss 302

One word is all you have to say: 'the Boss'. This is a car that makes you respect it because it can scare the hell out of you. That's exactly how Larry Shindola remembered it in an interview with *Mustang Monthly* in 1991. 'Ford was going to call it the SR-2 which stood for "Sports Racing." I thought it was a dumb name and suggested they call it Boss.'[78] Shindola viewed Ford's supervisors as conventional guys who couldn't relate to such a hip slang, but eventually the new name won them over. Ford's first Boss 302 rolled off the line on 17 April 1969, to be greeted by public and media accolades. *Car and Driver*'s opinion was that 'the Boss 302 is the best-handling Ford ever to come out of Dearborn and may just be the new standard by which everything from Detroit must be judged.'[79] Knudsen took the race replica concept to an entirely new street level.

From 1969 to 1971, Ford produced three Boss Mustangs – the Boss 302, Boss 351 and Boss 429, all SportsRoofs with high-performance engines and heavy-duty equipment, ideal for racing in the Trans-Am series, but Ford needed approval from the Sports Car Club of America (SCCA) for the revised 302 racing engine. A limited number of models equipped with the 302 or 429 had to be built for public consumption for the series to qualify as a racing model. The hood, rear deck, taillight panel (Cougar influence)

1969 Mustang Boss 302. (Clive Branson)

and grille area, where the headlights were mounted, were all painted black. Shinoda penned in some radical additions: a front spoiler that kept the nose almost licking the ground at high speeds, an adjustable rear wing and black rear window slats (a cool-looking but somewhat impractical addition). And Magnum 500 wheels carried large F60 x 15 Goodyear Polyglas tires that highlighted the exterior package. The muscle was controlled by a four-speed manual transmission and could go from 0 to 60 in under 7 seconds and cover a quarter-mile in less than 15 seconds. For reliability, the 302 was a rev-limiter that protected the engine from racing over 6,150 rpm. Horsepower is one thing on tarmac, but suspension is everything, so the engineers reinforced the suspension and shock towers to handle the stresses of high-speed cornering. The standard equipment list included front disc brakes, quick ratio steering, staggered rear shocks and colour-keyed rear-view mirrors. An imposing large graphic along the side featured Boss 302 lettering. Exterior colours were Wimbledon White, Bright Yellow, Calypso Coral and Acapulco Blue. Ironically, for all the effort in trying to humiliate Camaro, neither the Boss 302 nor the Camaro Z-28 dominated the SCCA's Trans-Am series. The two basically tied on the track, with the Trans-Am Camaro taking SCCA laurels in 1969 and the Boss 302 in 1970. As a tribute to their winning ways in the Trans-Am series, the street models are highly prized by collectors today.

## The Boss 429

Like the 302, the 429 was inspired by developments on the track. The Boss 429 was hastily built by Kar Kraft in Brighton, Michigan, to comply with NASCAR's regulations. To remain competitive, Ford had to get the 429 hemi-head engine qualified and the requirement was that you had to build a minimum of 500 production vehicles. Nowhere, however, did those requirements specify that a model and engine in question be built together, so Ford was very sneaky in making the Boss 429 V8 accessible as an option for street-going Mustangs, even for those that didn't qualify under the NASCAR specifications. It was unabated by the racing sanction. Muscle fans thought the Boss 429 would be the Corvette's Achilles heel, but were sorely disappointed. Instead, the Boss 429 merely existed for Ford to qualify 500 examples of its new racing engine for NASCAR. It was also the costliest non-Shelby Mustang experiment because the development required an expansion to the front suspension to fit the monstrous semi-hemi 429 into the bay.

Notable features included an engine oil cooler, trunk-mounted battery, power disc brakes, power steering, close ratio four-speed transmission, staggered rear shocks, manual choke and an operational hood scoop. The springs found on the 429 were the heaviest of any Mustang model and it was the first Mustang to have a rear sway bar installed. RAM-Air gave the 735-cfm Holley four-barrel better air to breathe, while header-type exhaust manifolds completed the look. Air conditioning and automatic transmission were forbidden as there was just no room. The exterior colours that were offered with the Boss 429 were Raven Black, Black Jade, Royal Maroon, Candy Apple Red and Wimbledon White and Blue.

The superspeedway-bound 429 got an A+ on high revs, but received a D- for standing-start acceleration. Moreover, the initial batch had faulty valve springs and sputtered at 4,500 rpm, instead of climbing to the correct 6,000 rpm peak. Ford built 1,356 Boss 429 Mustangs before ending its factory-racing program and retiring the car, whose promise and purpose never truly materialised. The Boss 302 fared slightly better, winning the Trans-Am in its second year, but it too was discontinued. They were both exceptional cars, and because of their short production runs, now command high prices at auction.

Whether Bunkie Knudsen was appreciated by Ford or not, he left an indelible imprint after his arrival in early 1968 and throughout 1969, as did the exaggerated designs from Larry Shindola. They were destined to pay dividends in 1970 and several years to follow, but Knudsen and Shinoda wouldn't be around to reap the rewards. Knudsen left Ford eight days after the release of the 1970 models, and Shinoda, who will be remembered for being instrumental on the robust yet stunning '69 Boss 302 Mustang, the '69 Boss 429 and the '71 Boss 351, was let go a week later. The writing was on the wall but Knudsen was illiterate. Iacocca recounts the times in his autobiography: 'Times had changed, he hadn't. He was a racing nut, but he failed to understand that the heyday of racing had passed.'[80]

## The Last Shelby Mustangs: The Swan Song

### GT350

It should be noted that 1969 was the year in which Carroll Shelby, designer of the Shelby Mustang and long-time Ford collaborator, lost control of the Shelby design. This resulted in his request for the company to no longer associate his name with the Mustang. Of course, by then it hardly resembled a Mustang. As a final goodbye, the GT350 and GT500 models were offered only in fastback and convertible versions. The fastback model used the Mustang Mach 1 body as its base platform. The last Shelby Mustang came off the production line in 1969 and by the end of the year, 789 cars had to be carried forward and renamed 1970 models, deceiving the public by painting twin black stripes on them. For the last call, the front-end styling was different from previous models. Lucas fog lamps were mounted beneath the chrome steel bumper, while someone must have had shares in scoops because they were everywhere – top, front side, backside, backwards and forwards. The fiberglass hood featured three forward-facing NACA scoops and four side panel scoops. The fenders had scoops to cool the front and rear brakes. Only 194 Shelby GT350 convertibles were built in 1969. Prices started at $4,753, almost $2,000 more than a standard Mustang convertible. If anything, it was the nail in the coffin for Shelby Mustangs.

### GT500

The 428 Cobra Jet continued as the standard engine for the 1969 Shelby GT500, which was available in both SportRoof and convertible. As an R-code Cobra Jet, the single Holley carburettor drew cooler outside air from the centre hood duct, while the other four openings contributed to lower under-hood temperatures. When ordered with the optional Drag Pack, the GT500 came with 3.91 or 4.30 gears, and the 428 was upgraded to Super Cobra Jet status with an oil cooler and strengthened bottom end.

Once the manufacturing of Shelby Mustangs was transferred to become an in-house operation at Ford, voices of dissent (and from those who were spiteful about Shelby getting the contract from the beginning) began asking product planners and management why the Mustang still needed Shelby's input; Boss 302 and Boss 429 models were being developed without outside influence, and their sales were beginning to catch up with Shelby's numbers. Others wondered aloud why they still had to manufacture them at all. Without much ceremony – and with few tears shed – Ford concluded it was going to end production of the GT350 and GT500 at the end of the 1970 model year.

## Cleveland Versus Windsor

Ford offered two hydraulic-lifter small-block 351-cid V8s for its Mustangs: one manufactured at its Cleveland, Ohio, engine plant, and the other at its Windsor, Ontario, facility. The Cleveland engine, the 351C, developed 300 hp at 5,400 rpm and 380 pound/ft of torque at 3,400 rpm. The Windsor engine, the 351W, produced 290 hp at 4,800 rpm and 385 pound/ft of torque at 3,200 rpm. Windsor and Cleveland were briefly listed together, causing more confusion. *Sports Car Graphic*'s Paul Van Valkenburgh wrote, 'Call up E&F [Ford's Engine and Foundry] to ask how many different engine designs they've built recently and they'll say, "You mean right now, or by quitting time?"'[81] The purpose of these engines was to appease the growing emission restrictions, but also keep performance credibility. Ford chose the Windsor engine, in which peak horsepower and torque arrived at slightly lower engine speeds, for the ever more elite Shelby Grand Touring 350s. Through the 1969–70 model years, Ford manufactured only 194 of the GT350 convertibles. In the end, the Shelby GTs went out with a whimper rather than the deserved bang as though it was being purged from the system. From Ford's perspective, the future was clearer (and possibly cleaner) now.

# 11

# 1970: Houston, We Have A Problem

After the onslaught of choices the year before, 1970 seemed mild in comparison even though bulk, size and speed were still a priority. Marginal changes took place and the engine options were whittled down to seven from eleven. In spite of the constant upgrades, Mustang sales continued to deteriorate, from when sales reached over 600,000 in the mid-1960s in a steady decline – 472,000 (1967), 317,000 (1968), 300,000 (1969) – to just over half that in 1970. Reasons for this were plentiful: government safety and emission restrictions (enforced by the 1970 Federal Clean Air Act), which would eventually kill the muscle car trend. As muscle cars grew exponentially in performance, so did the excessive number of car deaths (particularly with inexperienced young drivers in muscle cars), culminating in a stratospheric rise in insurance premiums, the soaring prices of muscle cars vying for more power and poor overseas sales (none of the foreign press liked the unwieldiness or discomfort of the muscle cars).

Though the Mustang outsold its main rival, Camaro, by 25 per cent, what good was this when the influx of foreign cars (which were smaller, more reliable and more economical) was now a real threat to domestic profits? Adding to the economic woes was the snowballing of gas prices. Ford was forced to take a step back and re-evaluate the future role of the Mustang. It had become too big for its own good and the original grace and élan that so attracted early admirers was lost. Legislation required auto manufacturers to develop engines that would eliminate 90 per cent of exhaust emissions within the next six years. It was an age of larger, safer bumpers and smaller, cleaner engines. Mustang was entering a less interesting but necessary new era of design and performance: one of pragmatism rather than prowess. This played right into Iacocca's hands, or so he thought. A displeased Iacocca summed up later: 'The Mustang market never left us, we left it.'[82]

With boss Bunkie out the door, and his ace designer with him in the recycling bin, Ford's Boss Mustangs, and all they stood for, were sure to follow. The Boss 429 assembly line came to an abrupt halt in January 1970, and Boss 302 production didn't survive the year either, though Ford engineers still managed

1969 Mustang and 351 motor. (National Automotive History Collection, Detroit Public Library)

to keep the hot 429 Cobra Jet big-block around for one last performance as the top muscle-bound option for Mach 1 Mustangs and die-hard fans.

## 1970 Boss 302 and 429

There were few updates. Mechanically, the '70 Boss 302 was identical underneath save for the addition of 1969's planned rear sway bar and a marginally increased front stabiliser. From the outside, colour choices expanded to thirteen selections, including the radioactive 'Grabber' series: Grabber Blue, Green or Orange. The black-out treatment was lessened on the hood and the Boss bodyside stripes, again made of reflective 3M material (for style and safety), were revised to run up over the fender tops and down the hood. Those old friends the Magnum 500 five-spoke rims were optional and the wheel covers remained flared. There was a weak scaffold of internal squabbles to continue the Boss series into 1971, but this was quickly opposed and vetoed by the upper echelon at Dearborn.

Except for the non-functional hood scoop, all side scoops were eliminated on Mustangs for a cleaner, more seamless streamline. The Kar Kraft works rolled out 857 Boss 429 Mustangs for 1969, then followed that up with 499 more 1970 models, but even with the introduction of the Hurst shifter, production eventually came to a sad demise. Ford's reasons for racing faded

1970 Mustang 428 Mach 1. (National Automotive History Collection, Detroit Public Library)

rapidly after Knudsen was sacked in September 1969, and the biggest Boss was among the first things to disappear as a result. It was arguably the greatest Mustang ever produced and broke all the rules for legal street car power. The 429 cid hemi-head V8 engine was so big that it needed to be shoehorned into an enlarged bay area and this could only be achieved when the car's suspension was altered. Ford even built a separate assembly line for this monster, but low production (859 fastbacks) reflected Ford's idea that the car was never a high priority, simply an excuse to race. Fifty years later, the Boss 429 remains one of the most sought-after Mustangs of all time.

## 1970 Mach 1 Twister

Ford made yet another version of the Mach 1, exclusively for dealerships in Kansas, called the Twister Special in ochre orange. The name referred to Kansas' notorious Tornado Alley, in an attempt to replicate the marketing success of the California Special GT Mustang. The 'C' graphic lines were removed for a single black horizontal line as well as the hood stripe, which was now one wide swipe. It also came adorned with black rear window slats (optional) and a black rear wing. The front grille received minor design cosmetic refinements – still blacked

1970 Mach 1 Ford print ad. (National Automotive History Collection, Detroit Public Library)

out but with dual headlights mounted inside the grille and no emblem of the horse. NASCAR pins were replaced with twist latches. The colour-coordinated racing mirrors, competition suspension and sport wheel covers remained the same as in the 1969 model. For racing, the Drag Pack option was offered with the 428 Cobra Jet RAM-Air engine, shaker scoop, engine oil cooler, beefed-up connecting rods and a non-spin Detroit Locker differential. Virtually nothing had changed from the 1969 version, except that the 351 Cleveland four-barrel replaced the rather long-in-the-tooth 390 FE series as an option. There was a lot of flash and plenty of zip, but regardless it was like gunning a car in quicksand as production sank to under 500 units. Insurance surcharges, hefty price tags and an oil crisis didn't exactly help matters. Only ninety-six Twister Special models were made in 1970, leaving them very rare.

## The Last Checkered Flag

Ford continued its racing program until November 1970, then pulled the plug, having just won the SCCA series manufacturers' championship, with champion Parnelli Jones and third placer George Follmer driving Mustangs for car owner/builder Bud Moore. Mark Donahue was sandwiched second,

1970 Mustang Boss 302. (Clive Branson)

driving an AMC Javelin. The Mustangs won six of the eleven races and finished second five times, but the sun was sinking on the muscle car; Knudsen was gone and there was no longer a need to produce a special Boss 302. Ford didn't completely abandon the muscle car theme and developed a high-performance, solid-lifter version of the 351 Cleveland for those remaining devotees. Even racing wasn't abandoned for long as Ford eventually returned to Trans-Am in the 1980s. In 1989, Ford captured the season championship with rookie driver Dorsey Schroeder, winning five out of fifteen races in a Roush Mustang. The 1997 Trans-Am season was totally dominated by Roush Mustangs, which won thirteen races, including eleven straight by driver Tommy Kendall.

# 12

# 1971: THE WRITING ON THE WALL

Henry Ford begrudgingly gave Lee Iacocca the top job as president in November 1970. To say that their relationship was tempestuous would be an understatement. They hardly talked to each other at work and were rarely seen together socially. Both could be volatile, impulsive and had enormous self-confidence – some might say hubris, one born of inheritance and neurosis, the other from spitefulness. Henry Ford was paranoid that Iacocca, backed by the loyalty of his disciples within the firm, had intentions on the company and actually initiated an in-house investigation of Iacocca, but couldn't implicate him in anything.[83] Iacocca, on the other hand, finally acquired the throne he had desired for years: boss of an automotive giant that employed

1971 Mustang convertible. (National Automotive History Collection, Detroit Public Library)

1971 Mustang Boss 351 convertible. (National Automotive History Collection, Detroit Public Library)

over 400,000 people, was building 2.5 million cars in the United States alone and produced over $500 million on a turnover of nearly $15 billion.

It is one thing to be promoted; it is another thing to inherit a monumental problem. Iacocca's cherished pony car of 1964 had grown into a Clydesdale by 1971. The Mustang hardtop, coupé and convertible were 3 inches wider and 7 inches longer than the original '64 model while dimensions meant 250 extra pounds – the largest weight gain in the car's history. Worse, the public still associated the new Mustang models with his name. The trouble with Mustang was that it had become a fat, masculine sedan. There was little Iacocca could do regarding the brand since the 1971 models had actually been signed, sealed and delivered back in the Knudsen's 1968/69 era to be rolled out in 1970/71.

The standard Mustang still retained the basic 250-cid inline, six-cylinder engine, but quite frankly its appearance was drab and anaemic and about as exciting as vanilla ice cream (this was to avoid the advertising of 'performance') by comparison to the healthier, sportier and tastier Boss 351 and Mach 1 – cars that Iacocca resented and Ford realised had to change in keeping with the times, but which had obvious sex appeal. The standard models even had nondescript dog-dish wheels. The only ostentation was a dual air scoop on the hood.

The Grandé was slightly better, wearing a new fully vinyl top like some fox fur boa around its shoulders with special emblems, like brooches, on the rear-roof pillars. The interior spoke of luxury with a two-spoke steering wheel, woodgrain appliqués on the dash, Lambeth cloth-seat inserts, electric clock and rear ashtrays. (Remember when people smoked?)

1971 Boss 351 sportroof. (National Automotive History Collection, Detroit Public Library)

For the last muscle hurrah, Ford redesigned the SportsRoof and introduced it as the Boss 351, superseding the defunct Boss 302. It was, not surprisingly, larger, but was less distinctive in appearance. Nevertheless it wasn't as temperamental, had better handling for its stature and, for a small-block engine, it had instant wallop. It packed a 351 cu. in. Cleveland V8 (R-code) punch, enabling it to throw its weight around with 330 hp at 5,400 rpm and 370 lb/ft of torque at 4,000 rpm. In other words, it was a wolf in sheep's clothing and with the assistance of a Hurst-shifted Borg-Warner T10 four-speed and a 9-inch differential with 3.91:1 final drive, it could outgun many of the big-block boys. This is not a car to sneer at. Its intestines consisted of a cast-iron unit of canted-valve cylinder heads and huge ports in the intake manifold, 750-cfm four-barrel carburettor, hardened pushrods, screw-in rocker studs, guide plates and forged aluminium pistons. All that sat on a beefy Competition Suspension package with reassuring power-front disc brakes.

1971 Mustang Boss 351. (National Automotive History Collection, Detroit Public Library)

A semi-gloss black hood was designed to reduce the sun's glare bouncing off and blinding the driver's view while rear window defrosters were introduced. The restyling of the back window made visibility cumbersome, but overall most critics gave it the thumbs up. Besides, there's no need to look behind when you're in front. Pony cars with big-block engines had all but disappeared, leaving a couple of stragglers behind trying to recapture glory days. Ford was surprisingly stubborn in relinquishing the Mustang's bloated size and remained so from 1971 to 1973. In 1974, as the Mustang's second generation emerged, everything was reduced to its original premise as an economic compact, without the sexiness, power or unique styling, designed by committee decision and computer analysis. Ford was never satisfied with one engine, and to displace the 429 there was the new, cleaner 385 series.

In 1970, Ford terminated its role in racing, and since the Boss 351 was now as popular at Dearborn as a gun is to a pacifist, it was discontinued halfway through the model year. *Sports Car Graphic* scribbled, 'Ford is now diverting all its racing talent and dollars into solving safety and pollution problems and trying to satisfy government mandates.'[84] While the Boss 351 isn't as popular as the Boss 302 or 429, it still has strong collectible prestige. And it has the credibility of being one of the fastest cars to emerge from Detroit in 1971. Only 1,806 Boss 351s were built before it was dropped, but it was a fitting tribute to Ford's Total Performance.

## 1971 Mustang Mach 1

The Mach 1 soldiered on into 1971 as the Mustang's sole fastback, the larger SportsRoof version with the tired 302 V8 base engine, but serious performance addicts could order the 370 hp Cobra Jet or, if you had deep pockets, a Super

Cobra Jet with dual RAM-Air to bump up performance to 375 hp. The flattened windshield, massive hindquarters and slopping roofline were so shallow that it was labourious to see behind when shoulder checking or backing up, and probably impossible had headrests been installed. The view was like looking through a mail slot. This was rectified in 1974 by the more conventional hatchback approach. The exterior displayed the usual treats: the honeycomb grille with the crest in the centre, new NASA-dual duct hood scoops, colour-keyed front spoiler/fender, dual racing mirrors (also in body colour), sport lamp grille, competition suspension, wheel trims with whitewall tires and a quick-release fuel cap, plus the accustomed stripes. Gradually all performance cars were losing their credibility as their size and horsepower were being seriously lowered to weed out the first generation Mustangs in preparation for a new crop more conducive with the environmentally conscious consumer.

1971 Mustang Mach 1. (National Automotive History Collection, Detroit Public Library)

# 1972–1973: End to an Era

It had been coming since 1968, yet most were either oblivious or in denial as cars grew larger and larger, as though the era of bulk and flex would continue forever. Like primordial creatures, these were cars whose rumble could go

1972 Mustang hardtop. (National Automotive History Collection, Detroit Public Library)

off the radar on a seismic graph, so it came as a rude awakening for Detroit to concede to government emission pressures. Gross horsepower and torque ratings fell significantly in 1972 – up to 100 horsepower or more – to meet such federal restrictions.

On the outside, one needed 20/20 vision to detect any difference from the previous year except for touch-ups on the make-up, like script lettering, but what lay under the hood was a different story. The standard Mustang engine remained the 250 cu. in., six-cylinder plough horse with the choice of a 302 small-block, two-barrel V8 (the NASA hood wasn't included), while its horsepower dramatically dropped from 210 to 140; a 351 two-barrel V8 (with the option of a RAM-Air addition); or a 351 four-barrel Cleveland V8, the latter available either as a 351 Cobra Jet (the largest engine for the year) or a 351 High Output (HO, a toned-down version of the '71 Boss 351), reducing 280 hp to 266 hp. Most of the engineering attention was diverted to the new crop of Mustangs emerging as the second generation.

The popular Mach 1 SportsRoof fastbacks still appeared invincible, as though they owned the street with hood scoops, competition suspension, front spoiler and rear wing, colour-keyed hood rear fender moldings, wheel trim rings and white-wall tires, but it was a bit of a facade with the underwhelmed 302 cid, two-barrel carbureted V8. The Mach 1 sales were 24.2 per cent in 1969, 21.5 per cent in 1970, 24.4 per cent in 1971 and 22.1 per cent in 1972.[85] Remarkably, sales increased without a major restyling effort to 26.3 per cent in 1973, proving the potency of power. In America, there could be a gas tank of fuel left in the country, and someone will demand a muscle car.

## Frozen Assets

To keep the faithful, Ford returned the Boss 351 as a one-off special model as well as introducing the Olympic Sprint package 'A' and 'B' cars, hardtops and convertibles decked out in the patriotic red, white and blue colours as a tribute to the US Olympic team for the 1972 Summer Olympic Games in Munich and the Winter Games in Sapporo. The Sprint package was purely cosmetic and there were no 'special' engine modifications or upgrades. But the marketing attempt was a bit of a bust. Fifty Olympic Sprint convertibles carried all the beauty queen candidates along Pennsylvania Avenue in Washington DC during the Cherry Blossom Parade, but no one informed Mother Nature, who dropped the thermostat reading to a bone-chilling 20 degrees fahrenheit. The potential princesses, exposed to the elements, turned different shades of blue and, once past the viewing stand, were whipped away with the ragtop covering them. After the procession, the cars were sent off to various dealerships as a high-profile blitz associated with the prestigious event, one that most would have forgotten or ridiculed. In total, only 800 Sprint models were produced.

## 1973

By 1973, the muscle Mustang was all but dead and simply living on a hospital drip bag. The media seemed to agree with Lee Iacocca that Mustang had strayed too far from its original concept. At least that was what was written, but Ford pulled a fast one and incredibly produced an even larger Mach 1 to accommodate a federally enforced bigger, impact-resistant front bumper. Surely this must be Ford's death march. The front bumper was a slab of

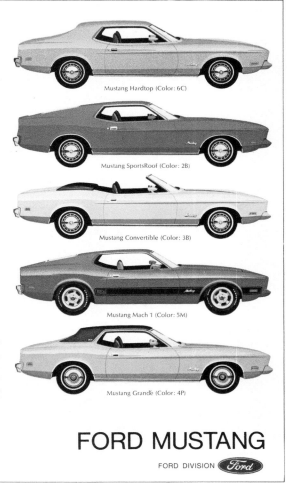

1973 Mustang collection (print ad). (National Automotive History Collection, Detroit Public Library)

polyurethane apparently capable of readjusting itself to its original shape on low-speed impacts, but closer to the truth was that it was cheaper to build than the traditional chrome version. Though this colour-coded fender blended in unobtrusively with the integrity of the car, it actually added 4 more inches in length. The so-called Mustang now weighed 900 pounds more than its 1964 ancestor. By trying to prove its masculinity, it actually alienated most potential customers. Because of its size and disproportionate styling, it was demanding to look out the back window and arduous to park. The only relief was that it was also offered as a convertible, so you could feel that you were driving a boat. The Mustang was now the only Ford convertible. In an uncanny move, the largest Mustang ever caused the greatest enthusiasm from the public. Derided by environmentalists as a gas-sucking abhorrence, the public assumed this would be the last convertible ever built by Ford, and flooded dealerships like a tsunami. More than 11,000 were sold in that final year. They weren't far off the mark as there was a dearth of Mustang convertibles for the next thirty years.

Basic Mustangs still used the conventional 250-ci/4L six or the 302 ci/4.9L two-barrel V8, while the more powerful 351-ci/5.75L selection ranged from a 177 hp two-barrel and a 248 bhp Cobra Jet four-barrel. Of course, the Mustang wouldn't be the Mustang without a surplus of options from minor details

1973 Mustang Grandé. (National Automotive History Collection, Detroit Public Library)

like a racy stripe package to a Hurst thruster or SelectShift Cruise-O-Matic transmission. But the size of the car wasn't the only thing that was impressive. This 351 V8 could pull off 266 bhp at 5,400 rpm and 301 lb/ft at 3,600 rpm. Not bad for something supposedly on its last legs. Regardless, a 'shortage of fuel' became a nationwide crisis and one of the first things to feel it was any obese, gas-guzzling monstrosity. The social scenario had become analysis against passion, life insurance against love. Consumers wanted fuel-efficient, small vehicles that wouldn't drain gas stations or their wallets. As a result, the ephemeral love affair with the muscle era came to an end. There were not even tyre marks racing off into the sunset: instead, they were buried in some garage or barn.

In September 1972, word through the grapevine was that the Mustang was developing into a radically downsized, fuel-efficient car, returning to its roots as a sporty compact pony car. The Mustang II was introduced two months before the first 1973 oil crisis and its reduced size allowed it to compete against imported sports coupés such as the Japanese Toyota Celica and the European Ford Capri. First-year sales in 1974 were 385,993 units, compared with the original Mustang's twelve-month sales record of 418,812, but it was certainly a better result than the muscle-car era. 1973 was the last year the Mustang was built on the original Falcon platform. The convertible model was also discontinued the same year and this marked the end of the first generation Mustang. Iacocca and Ford eventually parted ways in the late 1970s with Henry Ford's inimitable short parting words of wisdom: 'Let's just say, I don't like you.'[86] Iacocca was president for seven and a half years, holding the post longer than any other non-Ford family member. He had a glamorous and rapid rise to the top, usurping the role of vice president in his thirties when he headed Ford Division and became the golden boy when the Mustang was launched in the 1960s. The legacy of the Ford Mustang can be attributed to one man, Lee Iacocca and his vision and determination making the Mustang as American as apple pie and revolutionising automotive design in America with the advent of the pony car.

# 14

# SUMMARY

In 1978 Iacocca, having just been fired by Henry Ford II, was promptly swept up by the floundering Chrysler Corporation and became chairman in 1979. He got a quick fix from $1.2 billion in federal loan guarantees, then closed thirteen of forty-seven plants and slashed employment.[87] He introduced a car that Robert McNamara would have loved, the truly unimaginative K Car.

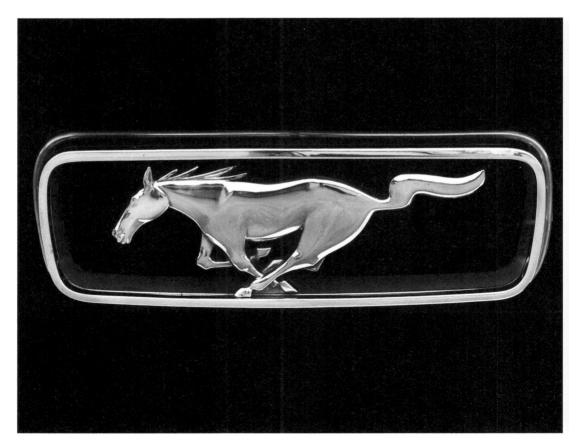

Mustang stallion emblem. (Clive Branson)

This car was so uninspiring that had it been held together by duct tape, it would have been an improvement. This vehicle made anything bland look beautiful, but it worked.

The word legend tends to be a misused term in an age of hyperbole, but the Mustang is truly unique based on its original premise: fast, fun and affordable. Though affordability is now questionable, it remains the essence and credence of the brand. As author David Geib states in his book *A Faster Horse*, 'The Mustang is a car line that has touched as many lives as the national anthem. It sold 22,000 units on its debut. Today's cars don't even scratch the number of Mustangs sold their first year.' Though Mustang sales have exceeded 9 million units worldwide, today Mustang is far less important to Ford's bottom line than its F-Series pick-up truck, but few car models will stir the soul or the blood of a loyal Ford customer more than the car with the galloping stallion on its grille. The brand symbolises everything that is exclusively American: power, freedom, individuality and confidence. It is an American icon, one that was honoured on its thirty-fifth anniversary in 1999 by the United States Postal Service issuing a stamp commemorating the original model.

The 2004 Mustangs were the final vehicles made at the company's Dearborn production facility, which had been building Mustangs since their debut. If you have Castrol oil for your blood, it is particularly difficult not to appreciate the endurance of the Mustang. The sound from its V8 alone is like poetry to the ears. 2019 is the Mustang's forty-fifth anniversary and no more fitting way to show appreciation then from those prophetic words of *Top Gear*'s former host, Jeremy Clarkson. 'This is a car that changed the world, mobilized a generation, redirected the way we thought about cars, and sounded like God shouting.'[88]

# ENDNOTES

1. Ikuta, Yasutoshi, *Cruise O Matic: Automobile Advertising in the 1950s* (Motorbooks International, 2000), p. 18.
2. Neil, Dan, 'The 50 Worst Cars of All Time', *Time* (2007), http://time.com/4723114/50-worst-cars-of-all-time/.
3. Farr, Donald, *Mustang Fifty Years: Celebrating America's Only True Pony Car* (Motorbooks Publishing Company, 2013), p. 6.
4. Mattoo, Shailan, 'Top 6 Lessons from the Ford Edsel Debacle of 1957', *Medium* (2016), https://medium.com/@shailanmattoo/top-6-lessons-from-the-ford-edsel-debacle-of-1957-8c0cb375443f.
5. Welch, Ted, 'The Emergence of the Pony Car', *Business Week*, 16 March 2006.
6. Farr, *Mustang Fifty Years: Celebrating America's Only True Pony Car*, p. 8.
7. Mueller, Mike, *Ford Mustang* (MotorBooks/MBI, 1997), p. 21.
8. Welch, 'The Emergence of the Pony Car'.
9. Ibid.
10. Ibid.
11. Mueller, *Ford Mustang*, p. 21.
12. Ibid.
13. Johnson, Richard, 'The bean counter who could have changed auto history', *Automotive News* (6 June 2016), https://www.autonews.com/article/20160606/OEM02/160609934/the-bean-counter-who-could-have-changed-auto-history.
14. Apple, R. W., 'McNamara Recalls, and Regrets, Vietnam', *The New York Times* (9 April 1995), https://www.nytimes.com/1995/04/09/world/mcnamara-recalls-and-regrets-vietnam.html).
15. Welch, 'The Emergence of the Pony Car'
16. Henshaw, Peter, *Mustang* (Regency House Publishing UK, 2005), p. 24.
17. Ibid., p. 25.
18. Newhardt, David and Lou Dzierzak, *Mustang Forty Year History* (Crestline/MBI Publishing Company, MN, USA, 2003). p. 12.
19. Henshaw, *Mustang*, p. 27.
20. Welch, 'The Emergence of the Pony Car'.

21. *Automotive News*, 'Lee Iacocca looks back at the 1964 sensation that was Ford Mustang' (12 April 2014), https://www.autonews.com/article/20140412/OEM02/304149996/lee-iacocca-looks-back-at-the-1964-sensation-that-was-ford-mustang.
22. Henshaw, *Mustang*, p. 27.
23. Healey, James R., 'Mustang: 50 years of daring moves, dirty secrets,' *USA Today* (16 April 2014), https://www.usatoday.com/story/money/cars/2014/04/16/mustang-50-anniversary-bill-ford-secret/6891965/.
24. Welch, 'The Emergence of the Pony Car'.
25. Newhardt and Dzierzak, *Mustang Forty Year History*, p. 24.
26. Henshaw, *Mustang*, p. 27.
27. Mueller, Mike, *Mustang 1964-½-1973* (MBI Publishing Company, 2000), p. 15.
28. Mueller, *Mustang 1964-½-1973*, p. 15.
29. Mueller, *Mustang 1964-½-1973*, p. 22.
30. Henshaw, *Mustang*, p. 28; *Automotive News*, 'Lee Iacocca looks back at the 1964 sensation that was Ford Mustang'.
31. 'The Man Behind the Pony – Phil Clark by Holly Clark', http://www.ponysite.de/phclark_mustangI.htm.
32. Welch, 'The Emergence of the Pony Car'.
33. Newhardt and Dzierzak, *Mustang Forty Year History*, p. 24.
34. Welch, 'The Emergence of the Pony Car'.
35. Murg, Stephanie, 'Quote of Note: Oliviero Toscani', *Adweek* (7 March 2014), https://www.adweek.com/digital/quote-of-note-oliviero-toscani-2/.
36. *Automotive News*, 'Lee Iacocca looks back at the 1964 sensation that was Ford Mustang'.
37. Welch, 'The Emergence of the Pony Car'.
38. Ibid.
39. Mueller, *Mustang 1964-½-1973*, p. 36.
40. Welch, 'The Emergence of the Pony Car'.
41. 'The Pony Car', Wikipedia, https://en.wikipedia.org/wiki/Pony_car. Also at 'An evocative event in California — 700 Mustangs appeared at a 20th Anniversary', *The Motor*, 166:25 (1984).
42. Newhardt and Dzierzak, *Mustang Forty Year History*, p. 16.
43. Farr, Donald, *Speed Read Mustang* (Quatro Publishing Group USA, 2018), p. 18.
44. Farr, *Mustang Fifty Years: Celebrating America's Only True Pony Car*, p. 29.
45. Welch, 'The Emergence of the Pony Car'.
46. Convert, Patrick, *Ultimate Mustang* (DK Publishing, Inc., 2001), p. 16.
47. Farr, *Mustang Fifty Years: Celebrating America's Only True Pony Car*, p. 32.
48. Ibid., p. 32.

49. Newhardt and Dzierzak, *Mustang Forty Year History*, p. 13.
50. *Automotive News*, 'Lee Iacocca looks back at the 1964 sensation that was Ford Mustang'.
51. Farr, *Speed Read Mustang*, p. 22.
52. Welch, 'The Emergence of the Pony Car'.
53. Ibid.
54. Ibid.
55. Ibid.
56. Farr, *Mustang Fifty Years: Celebrating America's Only True Pony Car*, p. 46.
57. Welch, 'The Emergence of the Pony Car'.
58. *Road & Track* magazine, 'The 1965 Ford Mustang Shelby GT350 was a Brute Back in the Day' (4 August 2015), https://www.roadandtrack.com/car-culture/classic-cars/a26269/the-1965-ford-mustang-shelby-gt350-was-a-brute-back-in-the-day/.
59. Mueller, Mike, *Mustang, the Complete Book of Every Model since 1964½* (Motorbooks/MBI, 2010), p. 86.
60. Dept. of Transportation (US) Motor Vehicle Fatality Rate, https://en.wikipedia.org/wiki/Motor_vehicle_fatality_rate_in_U.S._by_year.
61. Farr, *Speed Read Mustang*, p. 22.
62. Ibid., p. 104.
63. Mueller, Mike, *Motor City Muscle* (Motorbooks, 2011), p. 127.
64. Ibid., p. 12.
65. Ibid., p. 12.
66. Ibid., p. 127.
67. Ibid., p. 128.
68. Farr, *Mustang Fifty Years: Celebrating America's Only True Pony Car*, p. 55.
69. Mueller, *Mustang, the Complete Book of Every Model since 1964½*.
70. Ibid.
71. Ibid.
72. Levy, Emanuel, 'Bullitt (!968): Thriller, Starring Steve McQueen at his Coolest, and a Sexy Car' (7 February 2007), https://emanuellevy.com/review/bullitt-1968-4/.
73. Welch, 'The Emergence of the Pony Car.'
74. Mueller, *Mustang, the Complete Book of Every Model since 1964½*, p. 102.
75. Welch, 'The Emergence of the Pony Car.'
76. Mueller, *Mustang, the Complete Book of Every Model since 1964½*.
77. *Car Life* magazine road test, September 1969.
78. Mueller, *Mustang, the Complete Book of Every Model since 1964½*, p.122.
79. Ibid., p. 125.
80. Ibid., p. 142.
81. Van Valkenburgh, Paul, 'Ford Eats Ford', *Sports Car Graphics*, July 1969.

82. Henshaw, *Mustang*, p. 23.

83. Welch, 'The Emergence of the Pony Car'.

84. 'Air Pollution: We Know There's A Problem – Is there a Solution?', *Sports Car Graphics*, August 1970.

85. Mueller, *Mustang, the Complete Book of Every Model since 1964½*, p. 161.

86. Glassman, James K., 'The Iacocca Mystique', *The New Republic* (16 July 1984), https://newrepublic.com/article/90875/lee-iacocca-ford.

87. Grove, Noel, 'Swing Low, Sweet Chariot!', *National Geographic*, July 1983.

88. 'Ford Mustang – BBC World' [video], YouTube (uploaded 11 February 2015), https://www.youtube.com/watch?v=ITtiBYwWRb8.

# ACKNOWLEDGEMENTS

I would like to thank the following people for their permission to photograph their cars:

Sal Barakat, Mark Boyer, Luke Chin, Don Cook, Menno Dekleer, Scott English, David Harris, Keith Kehoe, Stephen Keith, René LaRochelle, Serge Lecours, Kim Lecuryer, Jeff Lott, Bruce McGill, Tim and Linda Nevras, Bob Richardson, Ross Saunders, Lyle Slater, Hub Steenbakker, David Truemner, and Kelly Tynkkynen. Furthermore, I would like to thank Carla Reczek for all her time and cooperation at the Detroit Public Library in supplying archival images for this book.